Working With Narrative in Emotion-Focused Therapy

Working With Narrative in Emotion-Focused Therapy

Changing Stories, Healing Lives

Lynne E. Angus and Leslie S. Greenberg

American Psychological Association • Washington, DC

Copyright © 2011 by the American Psychological Association. All rights reserved. Except as permitted under the United States Copyright Act of 1976, no part of this publication may be reproduced or distributed in any form or by any means, including, but not limited to, the process of scanning and digitization, or stored in a database or retrieval system, without the prior written permission of the publisher.

Published by
American Psychological Association
750 First Street, NE
Washington, DC 20002
www.apa.org

To order
APA Order Department
P.O. Box 92984
Washington, DC 20090-2984
Tel: (800) 374-2721; Direct: (202) 336-5510
Fax: (202) 336-5502; TDD/TTY: (202) 336-6123
Online: www.apa.org/pubs/books
E-mail: order@apa.org

In the U.K., Europe, Africa, and the Middle East, copies may be ordered from
American Psychological Association
3 Henrietta Street
Covent Garden, London
WC2E 8LU England

Typeset in Goudy by Circle Graphics, Inc., Columbia, MD

Printer: Maple-Vail Book Manufacturing Group, York, PA
Cover Designer: Mercury Publishing Services, Rockville, MD

The opinions and statements published are the responsibility of the authors, and such opinions and statements do not necessarily represent the policies of the American Psychological Association.

Portions of the case study material in this book are reprinted with permission from the following:

"Therapist Empathy and Client Anxiety Reduction in Motivational Interviewing: 'She Carries With Me, the Experience,'" by L. E. Angus and F. Kagan, 2009, *Journal of Clinical Psychology*, 65(11), 1156–1167. Copyright 2009 by Wiley-Blackwell.

"Margaret's Story: An Intensive Case Analysis of Insight and Narrative Process Change in Client-Centered Psychotherapy," by L. Angus and K. Hardtke, 2006, in L. G. Castonguay and C. E. Hill (Eds.), *Insight in Psychotherapy* (pp. 187–206). Washington, DC: American Psychological Association. Copyright 2007 by American Psychological Association.

"The Search for Emotional Meaning and Self Coherence in the Face of Traumatic Loss in Childhood: A Narrative Process Perspective," by L. Angus and B. Bouffard, 2004, in J. D. Raskin and S. K. Bridges (Eds.), *Studies in Meaning 2: Bridging the Personal and Social in Constructivist Psychology* (pp. 137–156). New York, NY: Pace University Press. Copyright 2004 by Pace University Press.

Library of Congress Cataloging-in-Publication Data

Angus, Lynne E.
 Working with narrative in emotion-focused therapy : changing stories, healing lives / Lynne E. Angus & Leslie S. Greenberg. — 1st ed.
   p. cm.
 Includes bibliographical references and index.
 ISBN-13: 978-1-4338-0969-9
 ISBN-10: 1-4338-0969-9
 1. Emotion-focused therapy. 2. Emotion-focused therapy—Case studies. 3. Narrative therapy. 4. Narrative therapy—Case studies. I. Greenberg, Leslie S. II. Title.
 RC489.F62A54 2011
 616.89'165—dc22
                         2011001777

British Library Cataloguing-in-Publication Data
A CIP record is available from the British Library.

Printed in the United States of America
First Edition

DOI: 10.1037/12325-000

Those who do not have the power over the story that dominates their lives—the power to retell it, reexperience it, deconstruct it, joke about it, and change it as times change—truly are powerless because they cannot think new thoughts.

—Salman Rushdie, *One Thousand Days in a Balloon*

CONTENTS

Acknowledgments .... *ix*

Chapter 1. An Introduction to Working With Narrative
            and Emotion Processes in Emotion-Focused Therapy 3

Chapter 2. How We Make Meaning:
            The Dialectical–Constructivist Model 19

Chapter 3. Facilitating Narrative Change Processes
            in Emotion-Focused Therapy 35

Chapter 4. Problem Markers: Same Old Stories, Empty Stories,
            Unstoried Emotions, and Broken Stories 59

Chapter 5. Meaning-Making Markers: Untold Stories,
            Unique Outcome Stories, and Healing Stories 81

Chapter 6. Working With Narrative and Emotion
            in Depression: The Case of Margaret 97

Chapter 7.	Working With Narrative and Emotion in Trauma: The Case of Alex	119
Chapter 8.	Conclusion	139
References		147
Index		157
About the Authors		169

ACKNOWLEDGMENTS

It is important to acknowledge the invaluable contributions of Emily Bryntwick and Tali Boritz, whose pioneering research on narrative and emotion processes in emotion-focused therapy have laid the empirical groundwork for the elaboration of the clinical research findings and intervention practices detailed in this book. We would also like to acknowledge the enduring patience and support of our closest family members, colleagues, and friends—you know who you are—who have provided us with continuous encouragement to make this book happen. Finally, with deep gratitude we acknowledge the important contribution of our clients for the development of our shared understanding of the importance of story and emotions in psychotherapy. We also gratefully acknowledge the contribution of Beth Hatch, whose wise and thoughtful edits helped bring our therapeutic work evocatively "to life." Thank you all.

Working With Narrative in Emotion-Focused Therapy

1
AN INTRODUCTION TO WORKING WITH NARRATIVE AND EMOTION PROCESSES IN EMOTION-FOCUSED THERAPY

Being human involves creating meaning and using language to shape personal experiences into stories, or *narratives*. Indeed, the sense of having a personal identity originates in the act of storying our experiences in the world so that they can be shared with others and reflected on for new self-understanding (Bruner, 1986). Our sense of security develops when we can, with the help of others, regulate our affect and weave a coherent account of our emotional experience with others. When we become narrators of our own stories, we produce a selfhood that joins us with others and permits us to look back selectively to our past and shape ourselves for the possibilities of an imagined future.

It is our contention that clients become narrators of their own lived experiences in psychotherapy when faced with a radically challenged sense of self and circumstance that no longer fits their "same old story." As Bruner (2002) suggested, by giving form to disconnected experiences and memories, narrative offers a space for self-reflection and self-construction, requiring us to interpret and make meaning of experience. As therapists, it is when we listen carefully to our clients' most important stories that we gain access to how people are attempting to make sense of themselves in the context of their social worlds. In this way, psychotherapy is a specialized discursive activity designed to help clients shape a desired future and reconstruct a more compassionate and sustaining narrative account of the past (Angus & McLeod, 2004a).

The role of client narrative expression has been addressed as a process diagnostic tool (Luborsky & Crits-Christoph, 1990) in psychodynamic therapy and cognitive constructivist psychotherapy (Dimaggio & Semeraris, 2004; Gonçalves, Henriques, & Machado, 2004) and is the focus of specific elaboration in Michael White's (2004) therapeutic approach to self-narrative reconstruction, narrative therapy. Only recently, however, has the interrelationship between narrative processes (Angus, Lewin, Bouffard, & Rotondi-Trevisan, 2004), such as autobiographical memory specificity, and deepened emotional arousal been empirically investigated in the psychotherapy research literature (Boritz, Angus, Monette, & Hollis-Walker, 2008, 2011). However, the specific client and therapist strategies that enhance narrative and emotion integration for productive therapeutic outcomes have not yet been identified in the psychotherapy practice or research literatures. These strategies are the focus of this book.

Although working with narrative processes was not fully elaborated in the early development of emotion-focused therapy (EFT; Greenberg, Rice, & Elliott, 1993), the two traditions share several theoretical assumptions and can greatly enrich each other in clinical practice. To begin with, as Sarbin (1986) noted, all stories are shaped by emotional themes. That is, stories help us make sense of our emotions. When we tell a story about a romantic experience, we use our emotions to assess what's "really going on" in the hearts and minds of our partners—in their inner world of intentions, purposes, goals, hopes, and desires. If we find a partner untrustworthy, we may attribute sinister motives to kind actions. However, the narrative organization of emotional experience allows us to reflexively understand what an experience means to us and says about us. At the same time, all emotions are shaped by stories (Sarbin, 1986). We feel happy or grateful when we create a narrative of a situation in which we see someone as having been kind to us. We feel angry or scared when we see others as intending to hurt us.

The authors of this volume have worked primarily in the two separate areas of emotion (Greenberg, 2002) and narrative processes (Angus & McLeod, 2004a) in psychotherapy, and in this book we have collaborated to develop a narrative-informed model of EFT (Greenberg, Rice, et al., 1993). We offer a *dialectical–constructivist model* that provides a dynamic understanding of how emotion and narrative processes (Greenberg & Angus, 2004; Greenberg & Pascual-Leone, 1995, 2001) contribute to effective therapeutic outcomes and self-narrative change. This model can be used to understand how people function in disorders as diverse as depression, trauma, addictions, and personality disorders, and it provides specific strategies for treating different narrative-emotion problems.

The purpose of this book is to provide clinicians with detailed guidelines, clinical examples, and empirical support for working with emotion and narrative in an integrated fashion. Throughout this book, we use several terms from EFT and narrative therapy that may be unfamiliar to the reader (see Exhibit 1.1).

The remainder of this chapter provides a broad overview of EFT, explains specifically how narrative work can inform the practice of EFT, summarizes the empirical studies that support our model, and explains how the rest of the book is organized.

BRIEF OVERVIEW OF EMOTION-FOCUSED THERAPY

One sees clearly only with the heart. Anything essential is invisible to the eyes.
—Antoine de Saint-Exupéry (1943)

EXHIBIT 1.1
Key Terms

Adaptive emotion: Immediate, biologically based survival-oriented affective response.

Emotional differentiation: Process by which a global emotional response is situated into its constituent parts in the context of a story.

Emotion scheme: An internal structure that organizes current emotional responses in terms of past emotional experiences and lived stories.

Emotion script: An emotionally based sequence that guides actions.

Lived story: Subjective experience of a lived event that has yet to be externalized as a "told story."

Macronarrative: Integration of personal stories to create a self-identity narrative.

Micronarrative: Individual personal stories disclosed in therapy sessions.

Maladaptive emotion: Immediate affective responses that have become dysfunctional in current situations due to past learning history.

Meaning-making marker: Client expression of puzzlement, confusion, or surprise in sessions.

Narrative scaffolding: Application of narrative schema for the organization of lived experiences.

Personal narrative: Representing lived experiences as told stories that unfold along a linear timeline with a beginning, middle, and end.

Problem markers: Performance indicators of underlying problems.

Process markers: Performance indicators of underlying experiential processes.

Specific autobiographical memory: Organization of lived personal experiences as episodic, imagistic events that are remembered over time.

Symbolizing: Articulation of felt or lived experiences in words or images.

Told stories: See *personal narrative*.

EFT views emotions as centrally important in the experience of self and in therapeutic change (Greenberg, 2002). It takes emotion as a fundamental datum of human experience and recognizes the importance of new meaning making and personal identity change for sustained treatment outcomes. Optimal adaptation is seen as involving a synthesis of affect and cognition, and the importance of narrative processes for adaptive emotion regulation and the emergence of new views of self have been increasingly highlighted in recent years (Angus et al., 2004; Elliott, Watson, Goldman, & Greenberg, 2004).

Although EFT (Greenberg, 2002; Greenberg & Watson, 2006), from its inception, has viewed the principle of human meaning making as central to effective therapy, the processes of meaning making in EFT have rarely been studied in detail (Watson & Rennie, 1994). In addition, the central tenets of narrative meaning making and identity formation were not explicitly included in the model. EFT grew from the humanistic and experiential roots of Rogers (1951) and Perls, Hefferline, and Goodman (1951), which included notions of an actualizing tendency to account for emotional health, whereas conditions of worth, or *introjects*, and incongruence between self-concept and experiencing were viewed as main players in dysfunction. EFT expanded these views by highlighting the role of adaptive emotion at the center of the actualizing tendency, the role of maladaptive emotion schemes in dysfunction, and the role of reflection on emotion in the creation of meaning and identity (Greenberg, Rice, et al., 1993).

In addition, EFT practice integrated elements of Rogers (1951) and Perls's (Perls et al., 1951) approach. *Being with the client* (i.e., being fully present and bringing specific relationship qualities to bear) was combined with *doing things with the client* (i.e., guiding the client through a process of change) to form a new style of practice (Greenberg, 2002). In this synthesis, following and guiding are seen as contributing to a synergistic flow in which neither person—therapist or client—always takes the lead or always follows. Relationship qualities include presence, empathic attunement, prizing, genuineness, acceptance, and validation of the client's experience. These relationship qualities are seen as the means by which the working alliance is established and maintained, as well as the means by which the therapist helps clients to engage with particular kinds of emotional processes for symptom reduction, interpersonal problem solving, and new meaning making. To these relational qualities are added marker-guided process directive interventions in which particular interventions, such as empty-chair and two-chair dialogue, are implemented when the client expresses markers of particular in-session problem states, such as harsh self-criticisms, during a therapy session. Informed by the contributions of Fritz Perls and gestalt psychotherapy (Perls et al., 1951), it is important for EFT therapists to be attuned when a client's more vulnerable internal voice—termed *the experiencing self*—is pitted against a more dominant voice—or *critic*—who bullies and harasses the experiencing self into silence. To facilitate a constructive dialogue between less dominant and more dominant internal voices—or *I positions*—EFT therapists are encouraged to help their clients identify, name, and externalize their critic and experiencing self voices in the context of empty-chair and two-chair interventions.

EFT is therefore an integrative psychotherapy approach, combining person-centered, gestalt, existential, psychodynamic, and cognitive theory, that fosters clients' emotional processing and regulation skills in interpersonal relationships (Greenberg, 2002) and that promotes heightened personal agency (Angus & Kagan, 2007) and an enhanced sense of coherence and well-being in life (Greenberg & Angus, 2004). EFT has been shown to be effective in the treatment of depression (Ellison, Greenberg, Goldman, & Angus, 2009), trauma and interpersonal injuries (Paivio & Pascuale-Leone, 2010), and couples distress (Greenberg & Goldman, 2008).

EFT's primary therapeutic goals are to increase emotional awareness and to transform maladaptive emotions into adaptive emotional responses that activate adaptive action tendencies and result in new story outcomes. The four different subtypes of emotional responses identified—primary adaptive emotions, primary maladaptive emotions, secondary reactive emotions, and instrumental emotions (Greenberg, 2002; Greenberg & Safran, 1987)—are assessed in an ongoing fashion while listening to clients' narratives in therapy sessions and guide differential interventions in EFT (Greenberg & Paivio, 1997; Greenberg, Rice, et al., 1993).

Primary adaptive emotions are the most fundamental, direct, initial, and rapid reaction to a situation and are accessed in therapy for their adaptive information and capacity to coordinate organized actions. *Primary maladaptive emotions* are also direct reactions to situations, but they no longer help the person cope constructively with the situations that elicit them. Rather, they interfere with effective functioning. Maladaptive emotional responses usually involve overlearned responses based on previous, often traumatic, experiences. For example, a fragile client may have learned when she was growing up that closeness was generally followed by physical or sexual abuse. Therefore, caring or closeness will be automatically responded to as a potential violation, with anger and rejection.

Primary maladaptive responses were adaptive in the original situation and often function as a kind of emotional survival strategy in reaction to the fears of loss, destruction of self, or humiliation and neglect that occur in our most important relationships. We have found that withdrawal emotions of fear, shame, and abandonment sadness are the more frequently occurring primary maladaptive emotions (Greenberg & Paivio, 1997; Greenberg & Watson, 2006). We have also found that primary maladaptive withdrawal emotions are transformed in therapy when clients are able to access primary adaptive approach emotions, such as anger, in relation to violation and sadness in relation to loss. However, it also appears that when primary adaptive emotions activate new ways of acting and being in the world, clients also report profound self-narrative change (Kagan & Angus, 2011).

In contrast, *secondary emotions* often function as reactions to and protections against primary emotional responses. These include feelings such as anger in response to hurt, or sadness that masks underlying anger. Emotional reactions to primary emotions also result in secondary emotional responses. For instance, shame can function as a secondary emotion in cases when a person feels ashamed of his or her sadness or anger. However, when clients shift from secondary reactive to primary adaptive emotions in the context of disclosing salient personal memories, the emotional trajectory of that narrative and its meaning profoundly changes. In fact, we believe that facilitating client shifts from a secondary reactive emotion to a primary adaptive emotion is a key narrative change event in EFT. At these moments, the essential emotional and psychological meaning of the story changes, and new perspectives on the experience of self and others in the context of the lived event open up for further reflection and understanding.

Finally, *instrumental emotions* are those that a person expresses to achieve an aim. These include crying or feigning embarrassment in order to appear appropriate. Instrumental emotions are emotional behavior patterns that people have learned to use to influence or manipulate others. For example, expressing shame to convey submission is often a cultural form of greeting. Instrumental emotion, however, can be dysfunctional when it is used rigidly and repeatedly to satisfy unmet needs.

A major premise guiding EFT intervention is that we cannot "leave" a place until we have fully "arrived" at it. We have to allow ourselves to fully experience what we are feeling in order to heal, and that transformation of maladaptive emotional response happens when we are able to access primary adaptive emotional responses. Therapists can help clients who are depressed access and experience their maladaptive feelings of shame or rejection by asking them to describe an autobiographical memory narrative in which these emotional responses have been strongly evoked. For instance, the client may be asked to imagine himself as a little boy who was all alone and to focus on what he felt and needed. He needs to arrive at this place before he can leave it. Transformation occurs when he is able to access a new emotional response to the old situation, such as when he first reexperiences his shame and fear as he remembers his abusive father and scenes related to the abuse, and then is able to generate new emotional responses, such as anger at violation, or sadness and compassion for the pain his younger self suffered. Transformation results in an expansion of the person's emotional response repertoire (Greenberg, 2010) that enables the expression of more adaptive action tendencies and a new story outcome.

Although feeling has to be felt to be changed, change involves more than just feeling an emotion. When EFT therapists can help clients arrive at their core emotional experience by disclosing, describing, and reliving events as told stories, clients can more fully differentiate emotions, access more adaptive emotions, and make narrative sense of their experience. In addition to heightening active self-reflection and purposeful meaning making (Angus et al., 2004), naming an emotion that is evoked in a specific situation or story—be it anger, frustration, or sadness—also has a self-organizing, calming effect that promotes a metalevel awareness of being informed by feeling states and being moved by action tendencies (Lieberman et al., 2004; Pennebaker, 1995). Too often, we underestimate the power of this simple action of situating and naming our emotion. In EFT, labeling emotions is called *symbolizing* or *differentiating* emotions.

EFT research shows that becoming an observer of your emotions puts you in the agentic position of having the emotion, rather than it having you (Angus et al., 2004; Greenberg, 2002; Greenberg, Auszra, & Herrmann, 2007). Once people start to acknowledge and differentiate hurt feelings or feelings of violation experienced in emotionally salient personal stories, it frees them to deal with them in different ways. For example, after naming and reflecting on the hurt of being neglected by a loved one, one can name the feeling of loneliness and the associated need for connection, and then one can either communicate this need or recall times when the other was more loving and supportive to reassure oneself of one's connectedness (Greenberg & Goldman, 2008).

In short, the fundamental purpose of EFT is to help clients better identify, experience, explore, story, make sense of, transform, and flexibly manage their emotions for the achievement of more satisfying intrapersonal and interpersonal outcomes. As a result, they become more skillful in accessing the important information and meanings about themselves and their world that emotions contain, as well as more skillful in using that information to live vitally and adaptively. The capacity to achieve emotionally meaningful, personal outcomes in life is an essential precondition for the emergence of more agentic and prizing views of self and the development of a positive narrative self-identity.

MARKER-GUIDED DIRECTIVE INTERVENTION

A hallmark of EFT is that therapists' interventions are sensitive to the in-session context of the therapeutic interaction, and particular client states are viewed as opportunities for facilitating specific types of client emotional processes. To date, six major types of marker-guided interventions have been identified and studied in EFT. The following EFT problem markers and their accompanying interventions have been identified (Greenberg, Rice, et al., 1993):

- *Problematic reactions* are expressed through puzzlement about emotional or behavioral responses to particular situations; for example, a client might say, "On the way to therapy I saw a little puppy dog with long droopy ears and I suddenly felt so sad, and I don't know why." Problematic reactions are opportunities for a process of *systematic evocative unfolding*, which involves vivid reentry into the situation to expand the person's narrative.
- An *unclear felt sense* arises when the person is on the surface of, or feeling confused and unable to get a clear sense of, his or her experience: "I just have this feeling, but I don't know what it is." An unclear felt sense calls for *focusing* (Gendlin, 1996), in which the therapist guides clients to approach the embodied aspects of their experience with attention and with curiosity and willingness to experience them and to put words to their bodily felt sense.
- *Conflict splits* occur when one aspect of the self is critical or coercive toward another aspect; for example, a woman quickly becomes both hopeless and defeated but also angry in the face of failure in the eyes of her sisters: "I feel inferior to them; it's like, 'I've failed, and I'm not as good as you.'" Self-critical splits such as this offer an opportunity for two-chair work, which is described in Chapter 3 of this volume.
- *Self-interruptive splits* arise when one part of the self interrupts or constricts emotional experience and expression: "I can feel the tears coming up but I just tighten and suck them back in; no way am I going to cry." These markers are opportunities for *two-chair enactment*, in which the interrupting part of the self is made explicit.
- An *unfinished business* marker involves the statement of a lingering, unresolved feeling toward a significant other, such as the following, said in a highly involved manner: "My father, he was just never there for me. I have never forgiven him. Deep down inside I think I'm grieving for what I probably didn't have and know I never will have." Unfinished business toward a significant other calls for an *empty-chair intervention*, in which the unresolved emotions are expressed to the imagined other in an empty chair.
- *Vulnerability* is a state in which the self feels fragile, deeply ashamed, or insecure: "I just feel like I've got nothing left. I'm finished. It's too much to ask of myself to carry on." Vulnerability calls for affirming empathic validation.

HOW A NARRATIVE PERSPECTIVE CAN ENHANCE EMOTION-FOCUSED THERAPY: CREATING NEW MEANING AND SENSE OF SELF THROUGH EMOTIONS AND NARRATIVES

We believe that an understanding of narrative processes in psychotherapy can inform and significantly enhance EFT practice in several important ways. Because emotion and narrative mutually influence each other (Greenberg & Angus, 2004), we believe that addressing both narrative and emotion processes is essential for achieving enduring, efficacious treatment outcomes in EFT. In particular, understanding that narrative expression is the basis for the construction of a sense of self, and that stories bring meaning to emotions, significantly expands the ways in which EFT therapists can effectively facilitate emotional change in EFT sessions. Our integrated model addresses stories that capture discrete events as well as an overall life narrative or story. Addressing discrete event stories is important when individual events are associated with trauma or interpersonal conflict, such as an assault or the discovery that a spouse has been unfaithful. It is often in the face of traumatic emotional losses and injuries, in which there has been a significant breach of trust, that clients find themselves unable to articulate an organized narrative account of what happened and to make meaning of those painful emotional experiences, because to do so would challenge deeply held cherished beliefs about the feelings, concerns, and intentions of self and others. For instance, when a middle-aged woman who has proudly defined herself as a loving wife and partner suddenly finds herself divorced—"dumped"—after 25 years of marriage, she is not only heartbroken but also her entire sense of personal identity and her understanding of how the world works are shaken to the core. Critical life events must be described, reexperienced emotionally, and restoried before the trauma or damaged relationship can heal. New meanings must emerge that coherently account for the circumstances of what happened and how the narrator experienced it, such that a plausible account of the roles and intentions that guided the actions of self and others can emerge.

Restorying salient personal experiences and the meanings they entail is also an important means by which self-narrative change and new views of self emerge in EFT. Drawing on the earlier example, the painful experience of an unwanted divorce that left the woman feeling like a failure may lead to a new understanding that she was not only a "good wife" to her husband, and undeserving of his actions, but also that she has always been a "good woman and person" who is deserving of love, respect, and loyalty in her most intimate relationships. Hence, narrative-informed EFT therapists should address the life story when the client's overall sense of self, or identity, is deeply challenged by painful interpersonal events and significant breaches of trust in relationships.

Life stories, or *macronarratives*, develop over time and continually shape and reflect the most important stories of our daily life. Although children recall single events that have had a particular significance in their lives (Habermas & Bluck, 2000; McAdams & Janis, 2004), young adults develop the capacity to make causal connections between events in their life unrelated in immediate time (Bruner, 1986). As such, autobiographical memory narratives are no longer simply referenced according to markers in time but also according to the emotions, motivations, goals, and attempts captured in the memory (Nelson & Fivush, 2004). For instance, as a 4-year-old, the experience of a house fire may be simply remembered by the loss of a cherished teddy bear. In contrast, at the age of 14, that same event may be recalled and disclosed as a fully differentiated story that now includes the terrifying emotional impact of the fire itself, the devastating loss of home that resulted from the fire, and the specific negative impacts that the fire had on the family, as substantiated by multiple memories that are integrated along the theme of a family tragedy. At some point, the meaning of being in a family that has experienced a significant tragedy will need to be addressed by the 14-year-old and will influence, in part, that teenager's view of self in the world. Macronarratives provide a perspective on how to evaluate, interpret, and morally evaluate important life events.

McAdams and Janis (2004) also suggested that it is during adolescence that core themes such as "a family tragedy" emerge that connect different life episodes together and serve as a coherent interpretive lens for understanding self and others (Habermas & Bluck, 2000). As noted in the previous example, autobiographical memories organized according to self-defining themes also provide us with a sense of who we were and who we are and give us a sense of purpose, unity, and identity. Hence, the capacity to narrate, understand, and integrate our most important life stories is key to adaptive identity development and the establishment of a differentiated, coherent view of self. Specifically, the articulation of a more coherent, emotionally differentiated account of self and others that facilitates heightened self-reflection, agency, and new interpersonal outcomes is a corrective emotional experience of self.

The terms *self-narrative* and *macronarrative* (Baumeister & Newman, 1994) have been used by personality researchers and clinicians to refer to the individual's development of an overall life story, perspective, or view of self and personal identity, in which discrete events are placed in a temporal sequence and meaningfully organized along a set of intrapersonal and interpersonal themes (Angus, Levitt, & Hardtke, 1999; Baumeister & Newman, 1994; Bruner, 1986; Howard, 1991; McAdams & Janis, 2004; McLeod & Balamoutsou, 2000; Polkinghorne, 2004; Sarbin, 1986; Singer & Blagov, 2004; Spence, 1982; White, 2004). For Bruner (2004), the sense of self originates in the embodied act of storying our lived experiences of the world. As such, it integrates the emotionally salient, lived stories and enables a sense of self-coherence and continuity over time. Once organized and externalized as a story, our subjective world of emotions, beliefs, and intentions can be shared with others, a storied "past" can be returned to for further self-understanding, and the hopes and dreams for an imagined future can be articulated. In this book, we use the term *macronarratives* to refer to overall life stories and the term *micronarratives* to refer to stories capturing discrete events.

McAdams and Janis (2004) suggested that no form of psychotherapy is likely to have a big impact on basic temperament traits, but a client's specific strategies, adaptations, and their internalized life narratives (i.e., macronarratives) have as much impact on behavior as do dispositional traits. In providing new macronarratives, therapists affect the personalities of individuals as much as they are changing the dynamics in families and other social relationships. Our narrative-informed EFT model integrates both emotion and narrative processes to create new meaning and sense of self. We refer to it as a dialectical–constructivist model because new meaning and sense of self are constructed through a dialogue, or dialectic, between different internal processes and between client and therapist. Chapter 2 presents the model in full, and subsequent chapters present techniques and case studies for applying it.

EMPIRICAL SUPPORT FOR OUR MODEL

There has been extensive research on the effectiveness of EFT (Greenberg, Watson, & Goldman, 1998; Watson, Gordon, Stermac, Kalogerakos, & Steckley, 2003). More research has been conducted on the process of change in EFT than in any other treatment approach (Elliott, Greenberg, & Lietaer, 2004), and the process of narrative and emotion change specifically has been studied and related to productive therapy outcome. A manualized form of EFT for depression, *process experiential therapy*, in which specific emotion activation methods are used within the context of an empathic relationship, has been found in three separate studies to be highly effective (Greenberg & Watson, 1998; Goldman, Greenberg, & Angus, 2006; Watson et al., 2003). EFT was found to be equally or more effective than a client-centered (CC) empathic treatment and a cognitive behavioral treatment (CBT). Both treatments with which it was compared were also found to be highly effective in reducing depression, but EFT was found to be more effective in reducing interpersonal problems than the CC or CBT treatment. It was also found to be more effective in promoting change in symptoms than the CC treatment, and it was highly effective in preventing relapse (77% nonrelapse; Ellison et al., 2009).

Angus and colleagues' studies of narrative sequences in EFT have revealed unique processing patterns associated with good treatment outcomes (Angus et al., 1999; Angus et al., 2004). Using log-linear narrative-sequence analyses, Angus et al. (1999) found that perceptual process (Toukmanian, 1992), EFT, and psychodynamic therapy dyads differed significantly from one another in terms of both the number of identified narrative sequences and the type of narrative sequences.

Types of narrative sequences include *external* (describing past and current episodic memories, or "what happened"), *internal* (identifying emotional experiences, or "how I felt"), and *reflexive* (creating new meaning, or "what it meant"). In the psychodynamic therapy sessions, a pattern of reflexive (40%) and external (54%) narrative sequences predominated. In contrast, the EFT dyad evidenced a pattern of internal (29%) and reflexive (46%) narrative sequences. Compared with the other two dyads, the proportions of internal narrative sequences were 3 times higher in EFT sessions than in the CC treatment sessions and 5 times higher than in the psychodynamic sessions. The primary goal of EFT is to assist clients in developing more differentiated and functional emotion schemes, and the evidence from these analyses indicates that this goal is achieved by an alternating focus on client exploration of experiential states (i.e., internal narrative sequences), followed by meaning-making inquiries (i.e., reflexive narrative sequences) in which new feelings, beliefs, and attitudes are contextualized and understood.

For its part, the CC therapy dyad revealed a pattern of consecutive reflexive narrative sequences (54%) occurring across topic segments in which clients and therapist engaged in extended reflexive analyses of both life events (external, 36%) and, to a lesser extent, emotional experiences (internal, 19%). Linking the reflective narrative sequences with other types of narrative sequences appeared to facilitate an extended client inquiry into core self-related issues in which automatic processing patterns were identified and challenged.

In a subsequent study (Lewin, 2001), good outcome EFT therapists were found to be twice as likely to shift clients to emotion-focused (i.e., internal) and reflexive narrative modes than poor outcome EFT therapists. In addition, good outcome depressed clients initiated more shifts to emotion-focused and reflexive discourse than poor outcome clients. Depressed clients who achieved good outcomes in brief experiential therapy were found to spend significantly more time engaged in reflexive and emotion-focused discourse than were poor outcome clients. These findings provide empirical support for the importance of emotion and reflexive processes in the treatment of depression.

Highlighting the importance of making sense of aroused emotion, process–outcome research on the emotion-focused treatment of depression has shown that both higher emotional arousal at mid-treatment, coupled with reflection on the aroused emotion (Warwar & Greenberg, 2000) and deeper emotional processing late in therapy (Pos, Greenberg, Goldman, & Korman, 2003), predicted good treatment outcomes. High emotional arousal plus high reflection on aroused emotion distinguished good and poor outcome cases, indicating the importance of combining arousal and meaning construction (Missirlian, Toukmanian, Warwar, & Greenberg, 2005; Warwar, 2005).

More recently, Boritz et al. (2008, 2011) directly investigated the relationship of expressed emotional arousal and specific autobiographical memory in the context of early, middle, and late phase sessions drawn from the York I Depression Study. Hierarchical linear modeling analyses revealed (a) a significant increase in autobiographic memory specificity from early to late phase therapy sessions and (b) that EFT and CC treatment outcomes were predicted by a combination of high narrative specificity plus expressed arousal in late phase sessions and that neither expressed emotional arousal or narrative specificity alone were associated with complete recovery at treatment termination. Specifically, Boritz et al. (2011) found that recovered clients were significantly more able to emotionally express their feelings in the context of telling specific autobiographical memory narratives than clients who remained depressed at treatment termination.

Adams (2010) tracked moment-by-moment client–therapist interactions and found that therapist statements that were high in experiencing (i.e., internal narratives) influenced client experiencing and that depth of therapist experiential focus predicted outcome. More specifically, if the client was externally focused and the therapist made an intervention that was targeted toward internal experience, the client was more likely to move to a deeper level of experiencing. Adams's study highlights the importance of the therapist's role in focusing on internal narrative processes. Given that client experiencing predicts outcome and that therapist depth of experiential focus influenced client experiencing and predicted outcome, a path to outcome was established that suggested that therapist's depth of experiential focus influences client's depth of experiencing, and this relates to outcome.

Another study on arousal examined the relationships between the alliance, frequency of aroused emotional expression, and outcome in the therapy of depression (Carryer & Greenberg, 2010). The frequency of expression data showed that a frequency of 25% of moderately to highly aroused emotional expression in most aroused sessions was found to best predict outcome. Deviation toward lower frequencies, indicating lack of emotional involvement, represented an extension of the generally accepted relationship between low levels of expressed emotional arousal and poor outcome, whereas deviation toward higher frequencies showed that excessive amounts of highly aroused emotion was negatively related to good therapeutic outcome. This suggests that having the client achieve an intense and full level of emotional expression is predictive of good outcome, as long as the client does not maintain this level of emotional expression for too long a time or too often. In addition, frequency of reaching only a minimal or marginal level of arousal was found to predict poor outcome. Thus, expression that is on the way to the goal of heightened expression of emotional arousal but does not attain it, or that reflects an inability to express full arousal and possibly indicates interruption of arousal, appears to be an undesirable, rather than a lesser but still desirable, goal.

Another study further distinguished between productive and unproductive arousal. In an intensive examination of four poor and four good outcome cases, Greenberg et al. (2007) did not find a significant relationship between frequency of higher levels of expressed emotional arousal measured over the whole course of treatment and outcome. They measured both aroused emotional expression and productivity of the expressed emotion and concluded that productivity of aroused emotional expression was more important to therapeutic outcome than arousal alone.

The measure of productive emotional arousal used in the study was further developed, and its predictive validity was tested on a sample of 74 clients from the York Depression Studies (Greenberg, Auszra, & Herrmann, 2007). *Emotional productivity* was defined as a person being contactfully aware of a presently activated emotion, where being *contactfully aware* was defined as involving the following six necessary features: attending, symbolization, congruence, acceptance, agency, regulation, and differentiation. These represent the ability to reflect on and generate meaning from emotion. Emotional productivity was found to increase from the beginning to the working and the termination phases of treatment. Working phase emotional productivity was found to predict 66% of treatment outcome, over and above variance accounted for by beginning phase emotional productivity, session four working alliance, and high expressed emotional arousal in the working phase. These results indicated that the productive narrative processing of emotion was the best predictor of outcome of all variables studied thus far.

EFT thus appears to work by enhancing the ways in which clients express their most important stories in sessions, which in turn facilitates a type of emotional processing that helps clients accept, experience, transform, and understand their emotions for the articulation of new narrative meanings and new story outcomes. This book emerges directly from both our ongoing empirical investigations of how emotion, narrative, and meaning-making processes contribute to productive treatment outcomes in EFT and our own direct experiences as EFT therapists working with clients in therapy sessions. Our intention was to integrate 20 years of EFT-informed psychotherapy research and practice and to provide psychotherapy practitioners, supervisors, trainees, and clinical researchers with a clinically grounded guide to working effectively with narrative and emotion processes in EFT sessions—and we hope that we have achieved this aim with this book!

ORGANIZATION OF THIS BOOK

This book consists of eight chapters. Chapter 2 presents our dialectical–constructivist model of narrative and emotion change. This model describes five key processing modes that facilitate new meaning making and self-narrative change. In addition, clinical guidelines for the implementation of narrative and emotion processing strategies in EFT are provided.

Chapter 3 provides an overview of how therapists can apply the model with clients. Two overarching therapeutic goals are identified: empathic attunement and changing narratives. Much has already been published on the former goal, but we have developed a unique approach to changing narratives. This approach involves retelling significant events, heightening client emotions, addressing limiting or incoherent narratives, and storying experiences of resilience.

As with the original conceptualization of EFT, our narrative-informed EFT approach is guided by *problem markers*, or outward signs of a particular problem to address. However, we identify new problem markers in the form of narrative patterns. Chapter 4 describes four common problem markers—same old stories, empty stories, unstoried emotions, and broken stories—as well as corresponding intervention strategies for productive meaning making and sense-of-self change.

Unlike problem markers, *meaning-making markers* indicate a new development in the client's self-story that requires therapist intervention for further integration and reconstruction of sense of self. Chapter 5 describes three common meaning-making markers—untold stories, unique outcome stories, and healing stories—that indicate opportunities for capturing and amplifying changes that have already occurred or are in the process of happening.

Chapters 6 and 7 provide in-depth case studies applying our model to clients with depression and emotional trauma, respectively. (Names and details for all clinical case examples have been changed to protect the anonymity of the client.) Finally, Chapter 8 summarizes key themes and addresses the implications of this work for clinical treatment programs and future research programs.

2

HOW WE MAKE MEANING: THE DIALECTICAL–CONSTRUCTIVIST MODEL

Life hangs on a narrative thread. This thread is a braid of stories that informs us about who we are and where we come from and where we might go.
—Anne Pellowski (1977)

Rather than viewing the client as independently constructing meaning, a narrative-informed emotion-focused therapy (EFT) perspective sees effective psychotherapy essentially as a coconstructive enterprise wherein the therapist is an important contributor to the meaning-making process (Angus & Rennie, 1988, 1989). EFT thus involves an interpersonal, dialectical process involving a synthesis of biology, culture, emotion, and reason that situates the client in a less radically independent, interior position vis-à-vis the construction of new story meanings and self-understanding.

This chapter articulates a dialectical–constructivist model of therapeutic change (Angus & Korman, 2002; Arciero & Guidano, 2000; Greenberg & Angus, 2004; Greenberg & Pascual-Leone, 1995, 1997, 2001; Greenberg, Rice, et al., 1993; Guidano, 1991, 1995; Pascual-Leone, 1987, 1990a, 1990b, 1991; Mahoney, 1991; Neimeyer, 1995; Watson & Greenberg, 1996; Watson & Rennie, 1994) that fully addresses the contributions of both narrative and emotion processes for new client meaning making and therapeutic change in EFT. The first section presents a theory of how new meaning is made. The section after that presents a clinical framework that draws on principles from the theory.

DIALECTICS OF MEANING MAKING: KEY PROCESSING MODES

Drawing on a dialectical–constructivist model of human functioning (Greenberg & Angus, 2004; Greenberg & Pascual-Leone, 1995; Greenberg, Rice, et al., 1993), a narrative approach to working with emotion suggests that EFT therapists are most effective when they are able to both follow and guide their clients' experiencing during therapy sessions and facilitate the articulation of new personal meanings. Specifically, our dialectical–constructivist approach to self-awareness and human meaning making identifies five key processing modes in which narrative and emotion are at play. The five overlapping—yet discernable—narrative and emotion-processing modes that support productive change in EFT are (a) awareness and contextualization of emotions, (b) symbolizing emotions, (c) narrative construction of emotional experience, (d) transformation of emotion and story outcomes, and (e) identity reconstruction. Each of these key processing modes or strategies is discussed more fully in this section.

Awareness and Contextualization of Emotions

The first key processing strategy involves paying attention to the bodily felt sense that arises from a situational experience, such as the body sensation of sinking and the action tendency of withdrawal associated with feeling humiliated by not being able to answer a question in a class of peers. This complex felt sense needs to be attended to before it can be symbolized. Gendlin (1996) informed us that the felt sense is of the whole situation. A complex bodily felt sense, for example, one that includes the emotion of shame about failure, also contains narrative elements such as the sequence of events, the desire to appear knowledgeable to peers and teacher, feeling the judgment of others, as well as the tendency to "want to hide and disappear." Our fundamental experience is coded first as a wordless narrative in imagistic sensory and kinesthetic form, and it is to this we must attend to turn our lived story into a told story.

The therapist thus works with clients to help them to attend to and become aware of their emotionally salient lived experiences in order to tolerate, accept, and eventually explicate and story their most vulnerable emotions of pain, hurt, anger, and rage in words for further reflection, regulation, and new meaning making. Awareness and acceptance of these emotions and the important meanings they convey about the intentions, goals, and beliefs of self and others constitute the first step in awareness work. Helping clients to narrate and then to subjectively enter and situate their most emotionally vulnerable and painful experience is a central focus of EFT.

Symbolizing Emotions

The next key processing strategy entails symbolizing and differentiating embodied feeling states now in awareness for new meaning making. Lieberman et al. (2004) showed that putting feelings into words (i.e., *affect labeling*) diminished the response of the amygdala and other limbic regions to negative emotional images. Regulation of underregulated emotion thus occurs through the ability to symbolize emotions so that the person is having the emotion rather than the emotion having the person.

To identify and regulate their emotional responses and cope effectively in interpersonal situations, clients need to symbolize their emotions, usually as words, embedded within a larger narrative context. Undifferentiated states of high emotional arousal—or what we will call *unstoried emotions*—are almost always experienced as disorganizing, distressing, and frightening by clients (Pascual-Leone & Greenberg, 2007). An important goal for EFT therapists, then, is to help clients symbolize in words the subjective emotional state they experienced in a particular situation, for further self-understanding. As shown by Angus, Lewin, Bouffard, and Rotondi-Trevisan (2004), the degree to which therapists are able to effectively guide their clients to an internal narrative mode of processing and enhance the symbolization and expression of emotion distinguished successful from unsuccessful EFT treatments in the York I Depression Study. It was the enhanced emotional differentiation of important personal stories that seemed to provide an essential experiential platform for productive client reflexive processing and new meaning making in clients who achieved significant clinical change at treatment termination.

This experiential (i.e., holistic) processing of emotions is different from conceptual processing (Epstein, 1984; Greenberg, Rice, et al., 1993; Greenberg & Safran, 1987). In experiential processing, the bodily felt sense acts as a constraint on the possible conscious conceptual constructions that can satisfy it, eliminating many other possible meanings. Because they are preconceptual, tacit felt meanings constrain, but do not fully determine, the narrative construction of personal meanings. Rather, felt meanings are synthesized with conceptual, often socially acquired, explicit meanings to form narrative descriptions of personal events (Greenberg & Angus, 2004; Greenberg & Pascual-Leone, 1995, 2001).

A crucial part of this meaning-making process is the production of linguistic distinctions to express this implicit bodily felt sense of meaning. In essence, naming an emotion integrates action, emotion, and meaning and provides access to the story in which it is embedded. For instance, one might symbolize a given internal sense as feeling tired or overwhelmed in the context of meeting an endless stream of demands at work. Both of these synthesized meanings of internal felt senses—tired and overwhelmed—convey different aspects of the same experienced situation in a way that, for example, *exhausted* or *afraid* would not. The words *tired* or *overwhelmed* are each adequate but capture different aspects of the total experience.

Conscious experience is not simply "in" us and fully formed but instead emerges from a dialectical dance that entails movement between (a) attention to an internal bodily felt-sense (e.g., "I am tired") and (b) reflexive differentiation and naming of that felt sense in the context of situational and interpersonal cues (e.g., "I am exhausted with meeting the endless stream of e-mails and requests for instant action at work these days"). Engaging in this dialectical dance helps clients to find words to capture and express the inner felt sense of a lived story as a told story that provides a platform for the differentiation of new personal meanings and self-understandings. How we articulate our feelings, most often in language and embedded within unfolding narrative frames, is thus crucial for the creation of new conscious experiential meaning.

Narrative Construction

The third processing strategy entails the conscious articulation of narratives in which symbolized feelings, needs, self-experience, thoughts, and aims are clarified and organized into a coherent story. Reflection on lived experience and its organization into an unfolding narrative enable the experience to be fully understood and accepted as part of a life story. Here, complex experiences, such as conflict or puzzling reactions, are organized into stories that are understandable and often new. For instance, understanding how a condemning self-critical voice leads to feelings of shame and helplessness helps clients to recognize the role they themselves play in maintaining their feelings of depression. Situations that previously evoked painful emotions can now be understood in a new, more agentic light that results in a deeper sense of experiential self-knowledge. Clearly, it is important to symbolize and express emotions in a narrative context. Our personal stories are given significance and salience when they become fused with emotion, and our emotions are given meaning when placed in their narrative context.

The reflexive system is a conscious, controlled level of emotional processing that generates *cooler* emotional representations (i.e., emotional representations with lower arousal levels) and provides higher level conceptualizations of who did what to whom. It creates a storied understanding of what happened, what was felt, and what it means. As established by Angus et al. (2004) in the context of effective EFT treatments of depression, the activation of the reflexive system appears to facilitate the organization and narrative representation of emotional experiences, which then enables the construction of an emotionally salient and meaning-filled narrative account of a person's self and interpersonal experiences.

Promoting reflection on emotional experience, as well as helping people make sense of their experience, promotes its assimilation into their ongoing self-narratives. It provides an understanding of what has caused the individual's responses and what they mean. The narrative contextualization of generalized distress states is also a highly adaptive emotion regulation strategy. Pennebaker (1995) showed the positive effects of writing about emotional experience on autonomic nervous system activity, immune functioning, and physical and emotional health. He concluded that through language, individuals are able organize, structure, and ultimately assimilate both their emotional experiences and the events that may have provoked the emotions.

People's self-reflections are generated both bottom up by emotional and sensorimotor processing and top down by conceptual processing in which self-understandings incorporate more socially acquired cognitive views that were obtained from others and inferred from past experience. Although often useful, these concepts may be sources of psychological difficulty. For example, views of self (learned conditions of worth; Rogers, 1951), or introjects (Perls et al., 1951), that favor image maintenance over experience interfere with here-and-now perception, whereas negative beliefs about self, world, and other produce much secondary distress. Whenever a personal identity narrative is overly controlled by these determinants, people are not grounded in their own primary experience, and emotional dysfunction may result.

Finally, the narrative organization of emotional experience enables people to coherently articulate and share their personal experiences with others and increases the likelihood of receiving support from others in times of need. In psychotherapy, it is our contention that effective therapists tacitly recognize the importance of both the implicit and explicit and selectively facilitate client shifts to the processing of emotion-schematic experiences and to fuller reflexive narrativization at different points in a bid to help them make conscious sense of their own emotional experiences.

Transformation of Emotion and Story Outcomes

The fourth key processing strategy involves helping clients change their basic implicit mode of emotional processing for the creation of new explicit meanings and story outcomes. Meaningful story change happens when a client shifts from maladaptive emotions, such as fear and shame, often in relation to traumatic life experiences, to adaptive emotions, such as anger and sadness at violation and loss of safety, which involves new stories (Greenberg, 2002; Paivio & Pascual-Leone, 2010). Now, rather than feeling self-condemnation, the aggressor may be held accountable or empathized with or even forgiven for his or her harmful actions (Greenberg, 2002). In EFT, a maladaptive emotional state and the meaning it conveys are transformed by activating a more adaptive emotional state. A shift to a new emotional response activates specific action tendencies that result in new story outcomes. As such, emotional change, by definition, involves narrative change.

In addition, a key narrative change event occurs when clients shift from expressing secondary feelings, such as reactive anger and blaming, to experiencing primary adaptive emotions, such as sadness and loneliness, which invoke new, more adaptive action tendencies. For example, in an initial EFT session, a young woman disclosed that she felt incredibly angry with her husband when he chose to spend time with his friends, without her. However, with further empathic exploration of key stories of loss and fears of abandonment in her childhood, she was able to access the primary adaptive emotion of sadness that accompanied her early experiences of loss. The shift from secondary maladaptive anger to accessing primary adaptive sadness provided the client with a new experiential awareness of how a long held, maladaptive fear of abandonment, and the deep sadness that it evoked, was triggering her feelings of anger and neglect in her marriage. This new emotional awareness also equipped her with a new understanding of the origins of her painful feelings of abandonment in her marriage and how they connected to experiences of loss in her childhood. She was now able to express her genuine need for deeper connections with her husband, without blame or resentment, which in turn enhanced her feelings of safety and security in the marriage. She also reported feeling less vulnerable when spending time on her own, and as a result, she was far less resentful of her husband when he chose to be with his friends.

Identity Reconstruction

A critical change process occurs when the client's most important personal stories and their emotional plotlines change. This final process involves different forms of identity transformation that result in the emergence of new self-narratives. In a recent qualitative analysis of posttherapy change interviews conducted with depressed clients at therapy termination, Kagan and Angus (2011) found that when clients are able to integrate distressing emotional experiences into a coherent self-narrative, one of two distinct forms of self-identity reconstruction occurred: (a) a new, profound sense of self-acceptance emerged in relation to preexisting views of self or others or (b) a radical reorganization of the self-narrative resulted in the articulation of new, more meaningful ways of viewing and understanding the self or others. In the former, clients found that developing the capacity to disclose, express, and story implicit primary emotions connected to painful, unresolved relationship issues resulted in a more compassionate view of the self and personal identity. In the latter, explicitly challenging self-critical processes in role-play interactions resulted in the spontaneous expression of new ways of feeling and being in the world that resulted in a sense of a "whole new me," as one client put it.

Importantly, the integration of emotion processes and narrative structure facilitates the construction of a storied explanation of what happened, which can then be told to others and reflected on for further understanding and personal meaning construction. Therapy then is a process of clients coming to know and understand their own lived stories and articulating them as told stories—and in so doing, changing their stories. In the process of articulating and reflecting on life experiences in psychotherapy, personal narratives become deeper (i.e., fused with emotional meaning and significance) as well as larger (i.e., taking more information into account and becoming more integrated). In essence, personal stories become both meaningful and meaning filled. The act of storying experience is an essential self-organizing process that provides a platform for subsequent reflection and personal meaning making in psychotherapy.

The term *autobiographical reasoning* refers to this type of narrative meaning-making activity. A narrative schema or structure organizes the ever-unfolding cacophony of lived experience into bounded episodes that by definition have a beginning, middle, and an end and enable perspective taking and reflection. Client narrative meaning making in psychotherapy is also viewed as evidence of increased client agency, in which clients come to see themselves as authors of their lives.

In a narrative-informed approach to EFT, the self is thus seen as being constructed continually, in an ongoing, self-organizing process. The self is best understood as an emergent organization of more basic elements. Embodied emotional experiencing and narrative organizational processes are both fundamental components of a higher order synthesis that ultimately determines who we create ourselves to be. Constructing a sense of self involves an ongoing process both of identifying with and symbolizing emotions and actions as one's own and constructing an embodied narrative that offers temporal stability and coherence. This process acts to identify one's experience as one's own and allows certain experiences to be seen as continuous within oneself.

A CLINICIAN'S GUIDE TO INTEGRATING NARRATIVE PROCESSES IN EMOTION-FOCUSED THERAPY

We now delineate four phases of narrative-informed EFT that provide a guiding framework for the effective application of the dialectical–constructivist processing strategies described earlier. These phases are (a) facilitating bonding, narrative unfolding, and awareness; (b) facilitating evocation, exploration, and articulation of narrative themes; (c) facilitating transformation of emotion and new story outcomes; and (d) facilitating consolidation and narrative reconstruction. Furthermore, key narrative-emotion tasks occurring within and across stages are distinguished by specific client narrative process markers. These *narrative markers* are outward signs of an inner state of interest in, and a readiness to work on, a particular problem. Markers help guide EFT therapists' selection of effective intervention practices for problem resolution (Greenberg, Rice, et al., 1993). We believe that EFT therapists can help facilitate productive narrative change by undertaking specific interventions to address different narrative-emotion markers that will be addressed fully in the second half of the book.

Phase 1: Facilitating Bonding, Narrative Unfolding, and Awareness

The initial phase of a narrative-informed EFT (Greenberg & Watson, 2006) involves the following steps: (a) attending to, empathizing with, and validating the client's feelings and current sense of self; (b) promoting the telling of the client's story; (c) providing a rationale for working with salient emotions and autobiographical memories; and (d) promoting awareness of internal experience and its narrative implications. A narrative-informed EFT involves an interpersonal activity rather than being a process in which a subject knower seeks to comprehend a client as an at-a-distance object. The basic experience of having a witness to one's account of troubles is meaningful and worthwhile. The role of the psychotherapist in this first phase and throughout includes being both witness to and coeditor of the stories told by the person seeking help.

From the first session, the therapist sustains a therapeutic attitude of empathy and positive regard with his or her clients to help create a safe environment for the evocation and exploration of emotions in the context of salient personal stories. A key mechanism of change in psychotherapy is the client's disclosure or externalization of emotionally salient lived experiences as told stories to enable further emotional differentiation and new meaning making in sessions. Client disclosures of their most painful and vulnerable personal stories in turn facilitate the development of a sense of trust and an emotional bond with the therapist that contributes to a strong therapeutic alliance (Angus et al., 2004; Kagan & Angus, 2011).

Narrative communication is basic for the emergence of personal acceptance in the therapy relationship. In storytelling, the listener and narrator are empathic partners and join in a collaborative alliance by their coconstruction of the client's narrative. Autobiographical memory storytelling facilitates the development of a strong, trusting therapeutic bond in which both client and therapist cocreate a sense of shared experiencing, knowing, and interpersonal understanding. The therapist puts or transfers him- or herself visually into the setting, the initial organization of the scene or the starting point of the story that sets up a series of unfolding events that invite a deepened experiential engagement in the client's story. The therapist's capacity to attend empathically to a client's key concerns, as conveyed in personal stories, contributes to an early development of a strong, secure therapeutic alliance by instilling a sense of basic trust in the client toward the therapist. The therapeutic relationship arises from a recognition that people find it helpful to have an opportunity to tell their story in a setting in which what they have to say is accepted and valued by others.

As Angus and McLeod (2004a) noted, there is a rhythm to storytelling during therapy sessions. Clients often talk first about what "generally" happens—what we call the *same old story*—which provides an overgeneralized description of problematic interpersonal relationships and patterns. EFT therapists help clients to access and disclose specific autobiographical memories that dramatize and make concrete and specific what is being talked about. In doing so, the person draws the listener (i.e., therapist) into his or her subjective, emotional world. Following the story, there may often be a period of reflection, evaluation, and interpretation in which the meaning of the story is explored. This process of sense making helps to develop a perspective on the "problem." There is also a rhythm within the telling of a story, expressed through repetition, contrast, reported speech dialogue, pace, and voice quality. Effective therapists are aware of the possible narrative trajectories that may occur during a therapy session and have expertise in facilitating client movement from one mode of narrating to another.

Narrative-informed EFT therapists pay particular attention to emotional stories and emotion in stories for further articulation and elaboration in psychotherapy. Emotions are "understood"—and have personal meaning for clients—when organized within a narrative framework that identifies what is felt, about whom, and in relation to what need or issue. Alternatively, unstoried affect may exert a disorganizing influence on personal meaning making and result in negative impacts on psychological (Dimaggio & Semeraris, 2004) and physiological (Pennebaker & Seagal, 1999) states. Emotion regulation is enhanced by organizing these experiences into a coherent narrative.

In the first phase of therapy, it is also necessary to provide clients with a rationale as to how working with emotion will help. This supports clients' collaboration with the aim to work on emotions expressed within salient personal stories. For example, the therapist might say, "Your emotions are important; they are telling you that this is important to you. Let's work on allowing them and getting their message." The therapist also helps the client start approaching, valuing, and regulating his or her emotional experience. The focus of treatment also begins to be established in this early phase. Therapists and clients collaboratively develop an understanding of the person's core painful narrative and work toward agreement on the underlying determinants of presenting symptoms. For example, when working with a depressed woman who had been a single parent for 5 years, the therapist, by following her pain, came to help the client focus on her underlying shame that came from her self-contempt for having married a man who had been physically abusive and for not having left him the first time he hit her.

In addition, overcoming avoidance of emotion often involves changing cognitions and beliefs about the dangers of emotional experiencing. Thus emotion-avoiding thoughts such as "Anger will destroy me," "Men don't cry," or "Emotions are irrational" need to be brought to awareness and challenged. Then clients must allow and tolerate being in live contact with their emotions. Hence, helping clients to disclose, subjectively enter, and situate their most emotionally vulnerable and painful stories is a central focus of narrative-informed EFT. The therapist works with clients to help them disclose emotionally salient lived experiences in order to tolerate, accept, and story their most vulnerable emotions of pain, hurt, anger, and rage for further reflection, regulation, and new meaning making. Acceptance of these emotions and the important meanings they convey about the intentions, goals, and beliefs of self and other is the first step in awareness work.

Phase 2: Facilitating Evocation, Exploration, and Articulation of Core Emotion Themes

The second phase of narrative-informed EFT involves the following four steps: (a) maintaining support for emotional experience, (b) evoking and arousing problematic feelings, (c) undoing interruptions of emotion, and (d) helping access primary emotions or core maladaptive schemes (Greenberg & Watson, 2006). During this phase, emotions are evoked and, if necessary, intensified. First, however, the therapist ensures the maintenance of sufficient internal and external support for evoking painful emotions. As noted earlier, trust, the ability to regulate, sufficient resilience, and the capacity to self-soothe all are necessary before evoking emotion. In addition to helping clients to approach, accept, symbolize, and tolerate emotions, emotions often also need to be regulated (Greenberg, 2002). It is important, however, to note that acknowledging, allowing, and tolerating emotion are important aspects of helping to regulate it. Helping clients to integrate emotional and narrative processes is an emotion regulation skill that involves such things as telling a trauma narrative, identifying and labeling emotions within the story, allowing and tolerating emotions, establishing a working distance, increasing positive emotions, reducing vulnerability to negative emotions, self-soothing, breathing, and being distracted. Soothing also comes interpersonally in the form of empathic attunement to affect and through acceptance and validation by the therapist. In narrative-informed EFT, therapists thus help clients contain and regulate emotional experience by providing a soothing environment. The ability to soothe the self develops initially by internalization of the soothing functions of the protective other (Sroufe, 1996; Stern, 1985). Over time, this is internalized and helps clients develop *implicit self-soothing,* or the ability to regulate feelings automatically without deliberate effort.

The goal of the evocation and exploration of emotion is to eventually arrive at the deepest level of core primary emotion and the articulation of core interpersonal themes. Many techniques can be used to do this, such as empathic evocation, focusing, and gestalt chair dialogues. Before activating emotion, therapists assess the client's readiness for evoked emotional experiences and ensure that the client has the internal resources to make therapeutic use of them. Once assured of this, therapists during this phase help people experience and explore what they feel at their core and articulate the organizing narratives at the heart of problematic identity and relational concerns.

Interruption and avoidance of emotional experience is also worked through in this stage. Therapists focus on the interruptive process itself and help clients become aware of and experience the cognitive (e.g., catastrophic expectations), physical (e.g., stopping breath), and behavioral (e.g., changing the topic) ways they may be stopping and avoiding feelings (e.g., therapist: "What's happening now? I see you tighten up." Client: "I'm squeezing my stomach and holding my breath." Therapist: "Yeah, do it some more to get a sense of how you do this"). Narrative incoherence and different blocks to narrative formulation, such as untold stories in which the client does not disclose a key part of his or her life experience and broken stories in which some cherished beliefs or hopes have been shattered, are dealt with by promoting narrative articulation.

Allowing a troubled person to tell his or her story (Angus & McLeod, 2004a) has a basic therapeutic value. From the story emerges a set of core therapeutic themes that are essential for the identification of and agreement on shared goals and tasks in the therapeutic relationship. In a study relating "on theme" depth of experience to outcome (Goldman, Greenberg, & Pos, 2005), core themes were defined as issues that are repeatedly discussed in therapy and that represent meaningful and important problems in clients' lives. Dominant themes for each therapy case under study were established by interviewing therapists at the end of treatment and asking them to identify what they saw as the mutually established major themes that had emerged through treatment that represented core issues. The interviewer also substantiated and elaborated therapist reports with information derived from client session reports. To help capture core themes, statements in client reports were specifically incorporated as theme descriptors. Based on this information, themes were established that were descriptive in nature rather than focused on underlying motivations or causative dynamics.

For example, one theme for one client was described as "lack of self-acceptance: client found it difficult being vulnerable and weak." She suffered from feelings of worthlessness and hopelessness. She felt she was "just unlucky." She felt vulnerable to threats from the outside world, experiencing only a "thin membrane" protecting her from attack. After gathering all the themes, such as this one, the investigators observed that themes fell into one of two overarching categories: clients' "view of themselves" or clients' "view of themselves in relation to the other." Themes were subsequently organized into these two categories, and it was found that all clients had at least one intrapersonal and one interpersonal theme. The theme identification procedure was found to be reliable in that episodes were correctly matched with themes (Goldman et al., 2006). Narrative themes established in this phase help organize the therapy and act to provide both the focus and coherence necessary for good outcomes.

Phase 3: Facilitating Transformation of Emotion and the Development of New Story Outcomes

The third phase involves emotional transformation and enacting new story outcomes. One of the most important ways of effecting productive client change in narrative-informed EFT involves helping clients change their basic mode of emotional responding (Greenberg, 2002, 2010). As noted earlier, the shift from primary maladaptive withdrawal emotions, such as fear and shame in relation to traumatic life experiences, to primary adaptive approach emotions, such as anger and sadness, which restore self-esteem and promote grieving for what was lost, promotes narrative change. Further emotional shifts from anger or sadness to compassion for the other leads to empathizing with or forgiving the offender for his or her harmful actions (Greenberg, 2002; Greenberg, Warwar, & Malcolm, 2008) or compassion for the self, in which one feels concern rather than contempt for the self (Greenberg & Watson, 2006).

It is important to note that the process of changing emotion with emotion goes beyond ideas of catharsis or completion and letting go, exposure, extinction, or habituation in that the maladaptive feeling is not purged, nor does it simply attenuate by the person feeling it (Greenberg, 2010). Rather, another feeling is used to construct a new understanding of an important lived experience and is the basis of narrative or story change. In narrative-informed EFT treatments, client change often occurs because one emotion (and the narrative meanings it conveys) is transformed into another emotion, rather than the emotion simply being reduced in intensity or extinguished through habituation. The client's same old story is changed by the activation of an incompatible, more adaptive, narrative that transforms the old narrative and the meanings it conveyed. In this way, emotional change is at the same time a narrative change. This involves more than simply feeling or facing the feeling, leading it to diminish. Rather, emotional change occurs by the activation of an incompatible, more adaptive experience that is storied and reflected on, and this new storied response helps transform the old emotional response with a new, more differentiated, coherent understanding of the self and others.

This view is supported by recent demonstrations of *memory reconsolidation*, which suggests that memories can be modified when they are reactivated (Moscovitch & Nadel, 1997). This theory proposes that each time an episodic memory is recollected or retrieved, a new encoding is elicited, leading to a new expanded representation or memory trace. Each time an event is recollected and reencoded, an updated trace is created that incorporates information from the old trace but now includes elements of the new retrieval episode itself—the *recollective experience*—resulting in traces that are both strengthened and altered. This altered trace may incorporate additional components of the context of retrieval, new relevant information pertaining to the original memory, or even new information that is generated during the act of retrieval. In this regard, memories undergo revision and reshaping as memories age and, most important, are recollected. The consolidation process results in memories that are not just stabilized and strengthened but also can be qualitatively altered by the recollective experience.

Changing emotion-schematic episodic memory structures most likely occurs through this memory reconsolidation process (Greenberg, 2010). An emotionally distressing event, such as a betrayal or abandonment, initially results in an emotional reaction. This emotional reaction to the situation will fade unless it is "burned" into memory by being formed into an emotion-schematic autobiographical memory. The more highly aroused the emotion, the more the evoking situation will be remembered (McGaugh, 2000); the emotional response can be recreated again and again long after the event. Thus, a memory of abandonment or betrayal, or something that reminds one of it, stimulates an emotional response of sadness or anger and hurt or fear in anxiety disorders and posttraumatic stress disorder and shame and sadness in depression.

Every time the memory is retrieved, however, the underlying memory trace is once again labile and fragile, requiring another consolidation period: *reconsolidation*. This reconsolidation period allows an opportunity to alter the memory. Maladaptive emotion-schematic memories can thus be transformed by introducing a new emotional experience during the period of reconsolidation. Thus, for example, feeling adaptive anger to overcome shame leads to changing the memory of the experience and, thereby, the narrative.

A primary goal of narrative-informed EFT is the heightening of client emotional arousal to facilitate shifts in client emotional processes. Emotion shifts can be in the form of movement from maladaptive emotions to more adaptive emotional responses or the accessing of new primary adaptive emotional responses in the context of personal memory narratives. Experiencing new emotional responses in the context of past life events can lead to significant shifts in the intentions, hopes, beliefs, wishes, and feelings that we attribute to the actions of self and others. At these moments, people see themselves and others in a new light and are impelled to construct a new, emotionally coherent narrative that accounts for what happened, why it occurred, what was felt, in relation to whom, and about what need or issue.

Phase 4: Facilitating Consolidation and Narrative Reconstruction

The fourth and final phase of narrative-informed EFT entails narrative reconstruction. New personal meanings are articulated in relation to the experiences of both self and others. At this stage, a conscious, causal explanation of experienced emotions is provided in the form of a new narrative account. Although Phases 1 through 3 address the interrelationship of emotion and narrative processes in the context of processing individual life events or micronarratives (i.e., emotions are put into narrative form and narratives are given significance by fusing them with emotion), in Phase 4 the experience is fully understood and accepted as part of the life story.

Macronarratives guide future actions, communication, and relationships and help us fit into our culture. We use these as standards to guide us, and they serve as templates against which to evaluate our own narratives. Satisfaction with our lives often depends on how events conform to our narrativized expectations. When our story breaks down our sense of continuity, coherence and control break down. Consolidation of coherent and new stories is thus an important part of the therapeutic change process and is essential for securing enduring change. As noted earlier, self-identity reconstruction in this stage occurs in two major ways: (a) the integration of a new narrative and new personal meanings into preexisting views of self or others or (b) the radical reorganization of the self-narrative and the articulation of new emotionally significant ways of viewing and understanding the self or others. When the emotional plotlines of their most important personal stories change, clients engage in the important final step of consolidating and integrating new experiences of emotional change as part of their self-identity narrative. It thus is critically important for therapists to facilitate active reflection and new meaning making about profound experiences of emotional change so that these experiences can be consolidated and integrated with existing views of self and others.

The question that arises in discussing narrative change is just how freely therapists and clients can restory and reinterpret events. Can each "picture" accept an unlimited number of reframes? As McLeod (2004) noted, narrative theorists have held two divergent views on this. Some theorists (Combs & Freedman, 2004) have maintained that there is a completely arbitrary relationship between events and interpretations. The strong position of social constructionism favored by Combs and Freedman (2004) takes a pragmatic view of truth as being whatever works to help a patient author a more life-giving reality for him- or herself. No one story has a greater truth claim than any other, but some stories are more "useful" than others. Combs and Freedman suggested that therapists and clients are always involved in the recursive loop of both anticipating future endings as well as going backwards to create coherent chains of significance that will ground potential outcomes. They argued that people produce chains of evidence to make the case they want to make and pick the clues according to what they have decided the mystery is.

However, we place more limits on the scope of interpretation, suggesting that events contain a range of meanings and emotions that can be attached to them and that therapists and clients do not have unlimited freedom to restory experiences; each picture can only accept a given selection of reframes (Greenberg & Angus, 2004). For example, we are not free to simply reinterpret an event or experience as one in which a personal loss did not happen or sadness is actually happiness. Our "constructivist" understanding of client change processes (Greenberg & Angus, 2004; Greenberg & Pascual-Leone, 1995, 2001) embraces the notion that meaning is a product of human activity and agency rather than an innate characteristic of the mind or an inherent property of objects or events in the world and that this activity acts to capture phenomena that do exist but are knowable only through our constructions of or actions on them. Thus, our model emphasizes that new meanings must be based on actual bodily felt experiences that are emerging from our lived experiences in the world.

CONCLUSION

Narratives serve to temporally sequence events; to coordinate actions, objects, and people in our lives; and to provide perspectives and meaning to our experiences. Stories of "what happened" constitute a discursive account of our identity as it emerges over time (Angus & Bouffard-Bowes, 2002; Angus et al., 1999; Angus et al., 2004; Hardtke & Angus, 2004), and the self-story is part of constructivist dialectic. It establishes a sense of the coherence and stability of the self by symbolizing patterns in experience across situations. It also provides discursive explanations for the sometimes inconsistent meanings and aspects of self that predominate in different situations and relationships. All of these efforts contribute to the ongoing life project of achieving a sense of self-understanding and identity in which the questions "Who am I?" and "What do I stand for?" are addressed. Given that the self is a set of complex self-organizations in constant flux, the creation of the self-narrative is crucial to the establishment of a stable identity. Narrative identity in turn is a complex consisting of a dialogical array of often contradictory self-representations whose underlying coherence is highly intricate.

We suggest that narrative interacts with the intricate network of bodily, sensorimotor, and affective subsystems whose information is organized and synthesized into experientially available self-states. This interaction is fundamental to embodied human experience and our sense of continuity. Productive therapeutic change is set into motion when clients are able to access, contextualize, and symbolize their emotionally salient lived stories as told stories for deepened emotional processing in the context of an empathically attuned therapeutic relationship.

3

FACILITATING NARRATIVE CHANGE PROCESSES IN EMOTION-FOCUSED THERAPY

This chapter demonstrates how to use narrative and emotion processes to help the client construct an overall life story that provides both (a) a secure sense of attachment that is sustained by the affect regulation functions of narrative ordering, contextualization, and symbolization of experience and (b) a coherent self-identity. When applying our dialectical–constructivist model to practice, therapists pursue these two goals to help clients develop new meaning and sense of self. This chapter discusses these two goals.

A SECURE SENSE OF ATTACHMENT AND AFFECT REGULATION

Childhood neglect and maltreatment is a significant source of affective dysregulation. Although difficulties in affect regulation often result from an ongoing lack of empathic attunement of infants' affects by caretakers, they also can result from intense emotional experiences at any point in life that do not receive adequate relational validation, care, soothing, and comfort. Experiences of abuse or trauma in which one feels violated, afraid, and powerless also can be major sources of dysregulation. People often experience emotional flooding as dangerous and traumatic, which leads them to try to avoid feelings altogether. At times, emotional avoidance or numbing may be the delayed result of trauma; this is one of the key forms of posttrauma difficulty.

In cases of childhood abuse, an abusing adult is often both the primary source of safety and comfort and a dangerous source of fear and humiliation at the same time. In such circumstances, the child's inability to be protected or soothed by the caretaker results in pathogenic states of anxiety, fear, shame, and aloneness. An empty sense of the self as unlovable, bad, defective, worthless, and helpless is formed. The self experiences despair, helplessness, and hopelessness. There can also be a sense of fragmentation, a feeling of falling apart, and an inability to regulate one's own affect. Thus, when a person who was abused as a child now feels fear of closeness, then emotions such as fear (once useful in coping with a maladaptive situation in the past) are no longer the source of adaptive coping in the present. Hence, the child begins to develop a pattern of insecure attachments that often brings him or her to therapy as an adult.

Importance of Therapist Empathic Attunement

Attunement to affect by an empathic, nonjudging other (i.e., therapist) and the experience of accessing, disclosing, exploring, and understanding painful and distressing life experiences with an empathic, nonjudging other (i.e., therapist) may constitute a corrective relational experience, one that can help heal patterns of insecure attachment and the attendant emotion dysregulation. Just as attachment researchers (e.g., Nelson, 1989) have identified how parents' soothing responses to emotion help scaffold and shape their children's narration of everyday life events, it appears that therapists' empathy also plays an essential role in helping clients to disclose their most vulnerable stories for validation and further emotional differentiation and new meaning making. Organizing lived experiences into a coherent narrative helps to regulate emotions. This is essential for the development of a secure sense of self and enables the articulation and communication of one's experience to others. The capacity to regulate and express emotions as a coherent story heightens the likelihood of being empathically understood by a listening other.

Specifically, therapists, through their capacity to empathically attune to clients' emerging emotional experiences, provide a safe and trusting space for accessing, disclosing, and reexperiencing painful personal memories. In addition, therapists help organize clients' painful emotions for further reflection by actively identifying specific situational contexts and cues that help contain, regulate, and explain emotional experiences. Therapists' use of scaffolding questions such as "Where do you feel that emotion in your body?" "When do you do recall sensing that feeling inside you?" and "Where were you when you felt that?" helps clients identify a narrative context for undifferentiated emotional experiences in therapy sessions. This strategy helps clients regulate painful affect as feelings become more understandable, specific, and controllable when organized within the context of a story. Alternatively, a therapist's empathic attunement to clients' overgeneralized representations of self and others—*empty stories* (see Chapter 4)—that are devoid of emotional feeling or tone can help clients to access and symbolize previously avoided emotional responses. This helps to bring new meaning to the events under discussion. Translating lived experience into told stories thus helps clients to regulate their emotion, and the empathic relationship provides a secure base in which this is achieved and helps clients develop a basic sense of security.

How to Experience and Express Empathic Attunement

Key elements of therapist skill in narrative-informed EFT are the ability to be empathically attuned to the client's emotions as he or she narrates the impact of events and the ability to express that understanding evocatively and effectively to the client. In essence, the difficult lingering emotions that a client struggles with when recounting distressing life events are seen not as problematic feelings in need of control but rather as opportunities to access and transform underlying maladaptive emotion schemes in the here and now of the therapy session. We believe that therapists need to help clients to disclose their most painful and vulnerable lived stories in order to help them tolerate, reflect on, synthesize, and restory previously avoided primary emotions and feelings. A therapist's capacity to responsively attune to a client's moment-to-moment needs for emotion augmentation or regulation during therapy sessions is key to the development of strong relational bonds and the disclosure of emotionally painful life experiences.

The quality and strength of the collaborative relationship between client and therapist in therapy—the *therapeutic alliance*—depend on developing and sustaining positive affective bonds between client and therapist and also on the collaborative aspects of the therapy relationship, such as consensus about, and active commitment to, therapy goals and the identification and implementation of specific tasks and interventions (Bordin, 1979; Horvath & Greenberg, 1989). On the basis of the empirical evidence that a strong therapeutic alliance is essential for effective psychotherapy (Castonguay & Beutler, 2006), alliance-building skills have become an important focus of intervention in our narrative-informed approach to EFT. In particular, we view therapist empathic attunement as a key precondition for helping clients to tell their story, which allows for the subsequent identification of shared goals and the introduction of tasks that, taken together, constitute a strong therapeutic alliance.

General recognition of the importance of a warm, nurturing relationship and the establishment of a secure emotional bond with a caregiver for adaptive psychological development dates back to Bowlby's (1988) views of attachment and to the Harlow (1958) monkey experiments. The pivotal role played by attachment patterns formed in childhood—particularly the experience of a safe, secure bond with an empathic caregiver—for the establishment of satisfying interpersonal relationships in adulthood has also been noted by many theorists (Ainsworth, 1979, 1989; Bartholomew & Horowitz, 1991; Bowlby, 1969). Psychotherapy researchers have established correlations between clients' recollections of caregiver relationships and clients' capacity to form an early working alliance in therapy (Mallinckrodt, 1991) and have identified the specific contributions of therapist empathy to the development of secure therapeutic bonds and productive outcomes in psychotherapy (Orlinsky, Grawe, & Parks, 1994).

As defined by Rogers (1975), *therapeutic empathy* entails the ability to (a) accurately attune to and perceive a client's internal, implicit frame of reference in terms of both conceptual and emotional meanings and (b) effectively communicate that understanding to the client during therapy sessions. Building on the empirical research evidence regarding the centrality of client narrative expression, and informed by the work of Rogers (1975), we view therapist empathic attunement as a key relational precondition for clients' disclosure and narrative accounts of painful and distressing life experiences in productive therapy sessions. For many clients, a primary impetus for seeking out therapy is the painful awareness that they do not have anyone in their lives to whom they can "safely" tell their personal stories. It is important to recognize that when clients feel understood and accepted by an engaged, confidential, empathic listener, they are also experiencing a new relational experience of interpersonal safety that increases the likelihood that they will share their most important and emotionally salient personal experiences with the therapist (Angus & Hardtke, 2007). The necessity to be known and to matter to another human being—to feel interconnected and attached to a caring other—is the fundamental impetus behind all personal storytelling.

Building on Rogers's (1975) definition of empathy, Barrett-Lennard (1986) suggested that empathic attunement entails a three-stage process. The first stage requires that therapists cognitively and affectively resonate with clients' descriptions of lived experiences. To achieve this goal, therapists are encouraged to track the unfolding plotlines of the client's told story while processing the affective meanings and impacts of those events—the tacit, lived story—at the same time.

Next, therapists need to evocatively communicate their affective and cognitive understandings of the client's lived story in the therapy session. As Angus and Macaulay (2010) noted, therapist-expressed empathy starts with the therapist sensing his or her own inner experience of a client's disclosure during therapy (e.g., "As she told me of her husband's tirade at the restaurant, I felt deep sadness, almost despair, about her marriage"). The therapist then tries to highlight and put into words the most poignant and implicit aspects of a client's experience on a moment-to-moment basis for further exploration and new meaning construction. A highly attuned therapist focuses clients' attention on experience just outside their awareness and thus offers meaning that disentangles and clarifies, and allows clients to explore further (e.g., "So as you sat in the restaurant, inundated by this torrent of criticism and complaint, it seemed as if you were drowning in despair, that this would simply never ever be different?"). The therapist phrases empathic communications tentatively, leaving the door open for clients to coconstruct new meanings and say if the therapist's empathic response fits their own experience of an event. Empathic explorations can be reflections or open-ended or direct questions to help the client expand on and differentiate his or her current experience. A therapist's attentive, concerned facial expression, forward lean, direct eye contact, and sensitive enquiring and tentative tone can all help convey empathic understanding. Finally, clients show perception of the therapist's empathic response (e.g., "Yeah, that's it; I wasn't angry, I felt sad and hopeless that our marriage *is* really over").

Finally, Barrett-Lennard (1986) argued that clients must *receive* or respond to therapists' empathic response such that they feel *known*—accepted and understood—by the therapist. It is the client's feeling of being understood and accepted by a reliable, nonjudgmental, and caring other that is the essential ground for the development of a positive therapeutic bond and enhanced client self-reflection and personal agency (Bandura, 2006) during the therapy hour. By facilitating the development of productive, client-focused processing outcomes, therapist empathic attunement also provides fertile ground for the identification of the shared goals and marker-guided task interventions that are essential for the development of a strong therapeutic alliance.

Sample Dialogues Showing Therapist Empathic Attunement

The following dialogue comes from a mid-therapy session with a depressed client. The therapist, by being attuned to the client's internal experience and communicating that understanding to the client moment by moment, provides a secure bond. This helps the client create narrative accounts of painful and distressing life experiences of aloneness.

Client: I can do it [get along] for a certain while, and but then—you know—you just, yeah, you do it for a certain while and then after a while you think, phff, why am I doing this? You know, I'm just, I mean you can be alone for a certain while. I think all people can, some people more than others. Like, I have no problem being with myself; it's when I know there's somebody out there, but when you're by yourself and you really feel that there's nobody out there, that after a while it starts to get to you.

Therapist: So let me see if I understand; I'm not sure if I misheard. You don't have a problem being alone if you know someone's out there. [Empathic understanding]

Client: Yeah, if you know . . .

Therapist: Yeah, yeah, so, then it's all right to be alone.

Client: Yeah, yeah, because you always know that you know you've got someone there to talk to or you want to go visit, or [*Therapist:* Yeah.] it's when you feel that there's nobody out there and you're alone then there's a difference between being alone and feeling lonely. [*Therapist:* Sure.] You know—that's when you start feeling lonely; you think, "Oh, jeez."

Therapist: So, your deepest kind of pain and fear is of being really all totally lonely. [*Client:* Mm-hmm.], meaning there's not even someone I can think of [*Client:* Right.] as being out there who I could contact, and then it's like this terrible aloneness, right? Yeah, and that's your sort of inner core vulnerability, it sounds like; it's like my parents were never really there, so I never had a sense of real connection [*Client:* Mm-hmm.], and then my sisters were my support, but it's different already [*Client:* Mm-hmm.]—you know they're not your parents. [Empathic reflection of a narrative theme]

Client: Yeah, exactly; that's exactly how it felt without anyone.

Therapist: So that somehow having someone there for you is very important [*Client:* Mm-hmm.], and when you feel like there's absolutely no one, that's the most frightening and terrible part.

Client: Mm-hmm, um, yeah, there are times, or there have been times in my life, where I have felt totally alone and—you know, I guess, you know—you say I'm a fighter and I am a fighter [*Therapist:* Yeah.], but sometimes I think what happens is—you know—when you're constantly struggling [*Therapist:* Yeah.], you get tired and that's when I think it happens. I get to the point where it seems like one bad thing after another bad thing, after another stressful thing after... And—you know—you wake up one day and you just think, "I can't do this anymore. I'm too tired. I'm tired of struggling to keep my life together." [*Therapist:* Yes, yes.] Last year was a prime example. I just got to the point where my life last year I just went, "I'm sorry." They kept telling me it was gonna get easier, it was gonna get better, and it's not getting easier. I'm 45 years old and it's getting tougher—you know? [*Therapist:* Yeah, yeah.] When I was 20, they said it'd get easier; when I was 30, they said it would get easier; and then when I was 40 and I just got the point that I just thought I just don't enjoy living anymore, it got...

Therapist: The struggle was too hard.

Client: Yeah, it was too hard. I thought to myself, "How do people in these poor third world countries do it? 'Cause they don't know any better? 'Cause they live in a hut and having dirty water and very little food and it's their way of life and they don't know any better?" [*Therapist:* Yeah, yeah, yeah.] Is that how? 'Cause I think to myself, "How do these people do it?" [*Therapist:* Right, right.] And why am I—I should—compared yourself to them, I'm in a much better [*Therapist:* Yeah.] state, I guess.

Therapist: But so it can just get to that point...

Client: Yeah, and it's just... I get to the point where you just become mentally and physically exhausted, exhausted. I would just, I would wake up and I would think, "Oh God, if I could only sleep and sleep."

Therapist: "I just want to sleep."

Client: Yeah, because then, of course, when you wake up, you start thinking [*Therapist:* Yeah, yeah.] there's all this stuff going on and you're thinking and you're thinking about your sister and you're thinking about that and you're worried about money and you're thinking about that.

Therapist: But somehow at the center of all of that is some sort of "I'm so alone [*Client:* Well, yeah.], there's nobody there for me." [Empathic refocusing on core theme]

Client: Yeah, and that's the way I felt last year: I felt like I had been totally abandoned [*Therapist:* Yes.] and that my life was going down the gutter and no one was reaching out to help and I was, I was amazed.

As evidenced in the foregoing clinical example, we believe therapist empathic attunement and expression result in the emergence of the following clinical outcomes in EFT sessions:

- A trusted relational bond provides a safe, interpersonal zone of exploratory inquiry that enables therapists to help clients disclose their most emotionally distressing, specific personal stories during the therapy hour (Angus, Lewin, Bouffard, & Rotondi-Trevisan, 2004) without fear of rejection or censure.
- Client engagement in active, self-reflection for the expression and symbolization of adaptive emotions (Greenberg, 2002) and core beliefs (Goldfried, 2003) is sustained by therapist empathic reflections and leads to the construction of new, more coherent and empowering personal meanings (Angus, Levitt, & Hardtke, 1999) and story reconstruction.
- Sustained client self-reflection and the emergence of new ways of seeing and understanding long-standing problems engender for the client a heightened sense of personal agency (Bandura, 2006) and self-mastery (Frank, 1961).
- Client expectancies for change and enhanced motivation for engagement (Westra, 2004) in therapy tasks and goals are established.
- Alliance ruptures are subjected to early detection and repair (Safran & Muran, 2000).
- The basis for a new, corrective relational experience (Castonguay, 2005; Pachankis & Goldfried, 2007) is established for the client.
- Client capacity for emotional self-regulation and strengthening of the self (Elliott, Watson, Goldman, & Greenberg, 2004) is enhanced during the therapy session.
- A new saliency and meaning to client experiences of positive change is developed (Hardtke & Angus, 2004; Kagan and Angus, 2011) along with the possibility of the emergence of insight (Angus & Hardtke, 2007; Castonguay & Hill, 2007) and a new, more positive view of self or self-identity (Goldfried, 2003).

The following clinical example, cited in Angus and Kagan (2009), specifically demonstrates how therapist empathic attunement and expression can help a client to disclose painful emotional experiences during an early therapy session. At the outset of therapy, Carol had been fearful that she would not speak fluently, honestly, and openly to her therapist about her most painful concerns, a pattern that also plagued her in many of her interpersonal relationships. Importantly, this core concern emerged in her initial therapy session, wherein Carol revealed to the therapist that she was deeply disturbed by the false front that she "showed the world." The experience of her own truth was different from the impression she was giving to others, and yet despite this awareness, she felt unable to make the shift to become more authentic in her own life. The following excerpt is drawn from Session 1.

Client: I am always giving that image to people that I am happy and I am OK, I am calm and I'm always—you know—good and helpful and kind and, I don't know, nice, but I know that there is something else going on; it's not the truth, you know. My image is different than . . .

Therapist: Than what's going on inside you. Right, so it's almost like you are the strong one; people come to you?

Client: Yeah, people think I'm strong—you know—and always have some solution. And—you know—I'm always happy because always I have a smile on my face. It's like I am the happiest person in my life.

Therapist: Right, right.

Client: But I know it's not the truth.

Therapist: So inside . . .

Client: Inside, it's opposite.

Therapist: So, it's kind of like this "you" inside here [indicates chest area] is saying, "I can't go on like this anymore"?

Client: Yeah, I didn't want to have that image—you know—of what I am showing to the world because it's not the truth what is inside me . . . It's, like, why I am playing this role? For whom?

Therapist: Right, for whom?

Client: And for what?

Therapist: And it's kind of like—what is it—I've been playing that for other people?

The therapist's expressed empathy and attitudes of nonjudgmental inquiry in response to Carol's most poignant concerns helped support and sustain her emotional disclosures. As Carol noted in her posttherapy interview, she was very "surprised" by the ease with which she was able to disclose her most important and painful concerns to the therapist:

I never experienced something like this, so I didn't know what to expect. I know for sure I was very scared of this . . . anxious—you know—how

I'm gonna—you know—talk or . . . if I can be open and honest with myself and with that person. And I think I got that, the courage to be open and to say what I really feel, or think.

We believe that Carol's positive experience of feeling courageous when overcoming her fears of accessing, experiencing, and disclosing painful feelings and beliefs during her therapy sessions constitutes an important corrective relational experience:

> I felt so free and without any fear or worries that I am not saying whatever I feel or I thought about it or . . . or some experience that I went through my life and that I could share it for the first time in my life with somebody.

The words that Carol used to discuss this important new development in her life are also significant: "I got that courage to be open." Her capacity to self-disclose to the therapist is a personal achievement that she has made happen by courageously overcoming deep fears of being judged or disliked and allowing herself to be seen and known by another, which constitutes a new interpersonal way of being.

The following excerpt was also taken from Session 1.

Therapist: Well, I really appreciate you being able to share these stories with me and the chance to see you, because that seems to be very important. It takes a lot of courage to come here and share these things.

Client: [Tearful, quiet] Thank you [softly].

Therapist: What's going on inside right now?

Client: I would like to be helped so I can be more myself or try to be more myself in interactions with people, so that I can find myself in this world, because I feel completely lost.

Therapist: I'm also hearing, "It's time." It feels like it's time.

The therapist demonstrated an early recognition of the importance for Carol of openly disclosing her personal feelings and concerns and validated the courage it takes for her to risk doing so. Carol was also aware of the significant relational impact that her therapist's empathic attunements had on helping her to access and explore emotional disclosures during sessions: "It was very important that she (the therapist) was with me, that she was with me. I found that she, she is really—you know, um—with me in the situation that we were talking about."

In summary, a therapist's capacity to empathically attend to a client's key concerns, as conveyed in personal stories, helps stories to unfold, and this contributes to an early development of a strong, secure therapeutic alliance by instilling a sense of basic trust in the client toward the therapist. In addition, feeling known and cared for by the therapist helps sustain a more secure sense of self for the client. Feeling connected to the therapist helps soothe feelings of anxiety and dread by breaking the sense of isolation. Over time, the empathic soothing of the therapist becomes internalized as a greater capacity for self-soothing and self-empathy.

Having established a secure base, narrative-informed EFT therapists in turn invite their clients to affectively and reflexively explore and expand on vivid memories in the therapy sessions. New meanings that emerge from the exploration of emotion and meaning schemes are then concretized by clients in the context of telling new stories about life experiences that represent new ways of seeing or interacting with others. In addition, it is through both the manner and content of client's narrative disclosures that therapists are able to discern problematic interpersonal patterns, maladaptive emotion schemes, and attachment-related communication strategies.

CONSTRUCTION OF A COHERENT SELF-IDENTITY

Narrative change in EFT has two main goals. As discussed earlier, the first goal is the establishment of a productive therapeutic alliance and a secure base that facilitates client disclosure of emotionally salient autobiographical memory narratives for further emotional differentiation, transformation, and reflective meaning making. The second goal is the facilitation of change in a client's expressed and internally perceived sense of identity and view of self. Given the core assumption that identity arises from narrative, it follows that revision to life narratives (Hardtke &Angus, 2004) is an important goal for sustained therapeutic change.

Therapy is essentially a process of clients coming to know and understand their own stories, and in so doing, changing them (Bucci, 1995). In the process of articulating and reflecting on life experiences in psychotherapy, personal narratives become deeper (i.e., fused with emotional meaning and significance) as well as larger (i.e., taking more information into account and integrating it). In essence, personal stories become both meaningful and meaning filled. The act of storying experience is an essential self-organizing process that provides a platform for subsequent reflection and personal meaning making in psychotherapy. The term *autobiographical reasoning* has been used to refer to this narrative meaning-making activity. A narrative schema or structure organizes the ever-unfolding cacophony of lived experience into bounded episodes that by definition have a beginning, middle, and an end and enable perspective taking and reflection. Clients' narrative meaning making in psychotherapy is also viewed as evidence of client agency, which is the source of new meanings in psychotherapy; for example, as clients actively engage in reflexive processing, making sense of their lived experience, they author their stories.

In a narrative-informed approach to EFT, the self is seen as being continually constructed as an ongoing, self-organizing process. The self is best understood as an emergent organization of more basic elements. Embodied emotional experiencing and narrative organizational processes are both fundamental components of a higher order synthesis that ultimately determines who we create ourselves to be. Constructing a sense of self involves an ongoing process both of identifying with and symbolizing emotions and actions as one's own and constructing an embodied narrative that offers temporal stability and coherence to these experiences. The constantly evolving sense of self operates as a synthesizing process, creating and being created anew in each moment and situation (Greenberg, Rice, & Elliott, 1993; Greenberg & Paivio, 1997; Greenberg & Van Balen, 1998; Perls, Hefferline, & Goodman, 1951; Rogers, 1959).

In summary, from a dialectical–constructivist perspective (Greenberg & Pascual-Leone, 1995; Greenberg, Rice, et al., 1993; Pascual-Leone, 1987, 1990a, 1990b, 1991), the reflexive construction of new personal meanings involves the narrative organization and articulation of felt emotional experiences. This is essential for lasting change experiences in psychotherapy. To better understand themselves, people continually symbolize, story, and explain themselves to themselves, and in so doing, construct an ongoing, emergent self-narrative that organizes their personal stories and provides a sense of self-coherence. In this manner, a coherent narrative identity emerges that effects an integration of reason, emotion, and action; that is, an integration of head, heart, and hand.

External, Internal, and Reflexive: A Narrative Processes Model of Self-Identity Change

To help therapists understand and facilitate client narrative change in psychotherapy, Lynne Angus and her narrative processes research team at York University developed the narrative processes model (Angus et al., 1999; Angus et al., 2004). In this model, accessing and articulating the client's world of emotions, beliefs, expectations, and intentions is critical for the emergence of new ways of seeing and experiencing oneself, one's losses, and one's long-standing relationship difficulties. The reflexive decentering from, and then reengagement with, distressing life experiences from different relational vantage points facilitates the articulation of new understandings about the self in relation to others. It is the reflexive processing of emotions, beliefs, hopes, needs, motives, intentions, and goals—and their inclusion in the events of the problem stories or narratives—that enables the experience to be fully understood and accepted as part of a coherent life story. A sense of personal or self-coherence is a global orientation that expresses the extent to which we possess a pervasive, dynamic, and enduring feeling of confidence that both our internal and external environments are predictable and that there is a high probability that things will work out as well as can reasonably be expected.

Given the core assumption that identity arises from narrative, it follows that revisions to life narratives will affect identity (Hardtke & Angus, 2004). The narrative processes model of therapy (Angus & Hardtke, 1994) contends that all forms of successful psychotherapy entail the articulation, elaboration, and transformation of the client's self-told story or macronarrative (Angus & Hardtke, 1994; Angus, Hardtke, & Levitt, 1996; Angus et al., 1999). According to the narrative processes model, identity is negotiated and renegotiated by the translation and externalization of lived stories into told stories as well as by the telling and retelling of emotionally salient events in one's life (Hardtke & Angus, 2004). Self-narratives are examined in therapy and different options for meaning making are explored and assessed by the client and therapist.

As noted earlier, in this model the self is cast as a multiprocess, multilevel organization emerging from the dialectical interaction between ongoing, moment-by-moment experience and higher-level reflexive processes that attempt to interpret, order, and explain elementary experiential processes (Greenberg & Angus, 2004). Narratives are classified as either *micronarratives* (i.e., client stories told in the therapy hour) or *macronarratives* (i.e., thematically organized micronarratives that constitute the client's life story). The thematic linkage of micronarratives is critical to the creation of the overall macronarrative. Within the narrative processes model, the therapist and client engage in three narrative process modes: external, internal, and reflexive. The following sections describe the different modes and identify therapist strategies for helping clients productively engage in these modes.

External Narrative Mode: What Happened?

In psychotherapy, it is crucial that clients remember and disclose emotionally salient memories and events to fill in the gaps in the narrative that may have been forgotten or never fully acknowledged and therefore not understood (Angus et al., 1999). This therapeutic process is represented by the *external* narrative mode of the narrative processes model, which addresses the question of "What happened?" (Angus & Hardtke, 1994). The external narrative mode may entail a description of either a specific event, a general description of many repeated similar events, or a composite of many specific events (Angus et al., 1996). Consider the following example:

Client: OK, it's been a pretty hectic week. My mother-in-law arrived in town. She'll be staying with us for 2 weeks. She's just taken over the house. She's cleaning everything. I mean, she even went out and bought Ajax and spent almost an hour scrubbing the kitchen sink. I mean it's not like the place was dirty; I made sure it was spotless before she arrived. The night before I even got up to check everything over so I could clean whatever was missed. She always does this.

Therapist: OK, your mother-in-law arrived for a visit and—what—the next day you walked into the kitchen, and she was cleaning your sink?

Client: Yeah, she arrived Thursday afternoon. R. [client's husband] picked her up from the airport. The next morning I dropped the kids off at school, and when I got back there she was in the kitchen scrubbing the sink—you know—with Ajax. So I just stood there with a dazed look on my face and said—you know—that she was on vacation and if the sink was dirty, I would clean it. Well, she said something like she knew I was busy and she was only trying to help.

Therapist: Mm-hmm.

Client: Yeah, and, like, she always does this.

In terms of the functions of spoken narratives, we argue that in the external sequences, the narrator or client attempts to verbally show the therapist—by means of descriptive, specific details—the scene, setting, and actions in an event. The disclosure of autobiographical memory narratives, in the context of the external narrative mode, provides the client with the chance to engage in storytelling and to create a visually rich picture for the therapist by means of verbally descriptive and specific details of life experiences and events (Angus et al., 1999). The more detailed and specific the description provided by the client, the more opportunity the therapist has to develop an imagistic rendering of the event and to empathically adopt the client's internal frame. Hence, therapists intentionally shift clients into an external narrative sequence by asking them to give a detailed concrete example or life event to exemplify a general concern or issue and to facilitate a reexperiencing, as opposed to a retelling, of past memories and significant events.

Internal Narrative Mode: What Do I Feel?

Clients also need to be fully engaged in the lived experience of an event to bring to awareness, and fully articulate, tacit feelings and emotions. This is achieved by both the therapist and client engaging in the detailed unfolding and exploration of associated sensations and emotions that emerge in the retelling of an autobiographical memory. The *internal* narrative process mode entails the description and elaboration of subjective feelings, reactions, and emotions connected with an event and addresses the question of "What do I feel?" during the event. In addition, the internal narrative mode addresses what was felt in relation to the event during the therapy session. Consider the following example:

Therapist: Mm-hmm. So, how does it make you feel when she acts like this?

Client: I feel like she's intruding. I mean, she's the guest. I don't know; I just want to scream, I get so frustrated. She makes me feel hopeless, like a little kid. There is no point telling R.; he just sides with her. I just get really upset, just feel like one of the kids when she's around.

Therapist: Mm-hmm. So, when she visits, you feel like she is the parent and you're the little kid?

Client: Yeah, like when she cleans or says that I'm not dressing my kids right, I feel like I've failed again. It is so aggravating. No matter how hard I try I can't please her. I think I'm starting to experience panic attacks when I know she's coming for a visit.

Therapist: Panic attacks?

Client: Like, before she arrived, I had a headache for a week. My stomach was in a knot, and I could hardly eat. I just felt really tense and nervous. I just know that she will find something to criticize me about.

Therapist: Mm-hmm.

The function of the internal mode of inquiry for the client is to share with the therapist his or her reexperienced feelings and emotions that are associated with the retelling of a particular event (external mode) and to articulate newly emerging feelings and emotions occurring during the therapy hour (Angus et al., 1999). Feelings, once accessed and symbolized, are made sense of and transformed by the incorporation of new experience from newly accessed adaptive feelings and needs (Greenberg, 2010). Research also supports the notion that emotional disclosure regarding traumatic events can result in positive immunological and psychological effects for survivors

(Harber & Pennebaker, 1992; Pennebaker & Seagal, 1999). In the context of dealing with physical and psychological trauma, Harber and Pennebaker (1992) provided compelling research findings that demonstrated that emotional disclosure in the context of trauma narratives is predictive of positive immune system response in survivors.

Reflexive Narrative Mode: What Does It Mean?

New meaning is constructed through the reflexive analysis of articulated experiences. Clients explore personal expectations, needs, motivations, anticipations, and beliefs of both the self and other in the context of their personal stories and attempt to make meaning of those experiences. The reflexive narrative process mode addresses the question "What does it mean?" in relation to what happened and what was felt during an event. By reflexively processing current and past experiences, the client and therapist begin to coconstruct a meaningful framework of understanding, or macronarrative, which coherently organizes and provides an understanding of the client's current and past experiences in the world. Consider the following example:

Client: And I don't know why I feel so obsessed with pleasing her anyway. She usually only comes to visit twice a year. I mean, it's not like we're really close. I've talked to R, who says I should just put up with her for 2 weeks then forget about her, but I can't seem to do that. Maybe it's because I felt she never thought much of me. She was against R. and I marrying. We were still in school. She's always given me the impression that she thought R. would marry someone who would be more than a housewife. Why don't I have the guts to stand up to her? Why do I let her invade my home? I always let her take charge. I should stand up for myself and tell her what I think about all her cleaning. Maybe it I stood up to her, she'd respect me more, or at least she might shut up!

Greenberg and Angus (2004), citing findings from Pennebaker's (1995) work with trauma survivors, argued that reflexive elaboration and meaning creation can be important therapeutic consequences of client emotional expression if the therapist actively facilitates the client's focusing on the creation of new meaning (i.e., reflexive narrative sequence) from the aroused emotional material (i.e., internal narrative sequence). Reflexive narrative processing that does not emerge from the detailed description of events and emotional expression may be a client marker of shallow, automated processing (Borkovec, Roemer, & Kinyon, 1995) in which the client appears to be retelling a well-rehearsed script. By asking for a specific example of the problem or concern, hence shifting the client to describing and showing a specific instance (i.e., external narrative sequence), the therapist may help the client to engage in a kind of depth of internal and reflexive narrative processing such that deeply painful, and at times disturbing, feelings and beliefs about the self can be articulated and understood in ways that engender new meanings and perspectives on self and others. This reconstructed narrative may either support or challenge the implicit beliefs about self and others, which contribute to the client's life story or macronarrative (Angus & Bouffard, 2004). The reflexive narrative mode represents this therapeutic process and is characterized as the reflexive analyses of events and subjective feelings. Therefore, this narrative process mode addresses the question "What does it mean?" in relation to what happened or what was felt during an event.

Shifting Between Modes

From a narrative processes model perspective, it is the client's narrative description of emotionally salient, autobiographical memory narratives—*external narrative sequences*—that provides the essential experiential starting point for reflexive processing of evoked emotions and the subsequent articulation of related personal meanings. It is our view that emergent personal meanings arising from the processing of adaptive emotions exist within a tacit narrative schema in which a new story emerges to account for what was felt, in relation to whom, and about what need or concern. Moreover, when emotions shift, clients are impelled to articulate and story the new emotional landscape they find themselves inhabiting. New views of self and other in terms of probable intentions, beliefs, and goals also shift and change in the quest to create an emotionally coherent story.

One of the unique insights generated by studies that tracked narrative process sequence change in during EFT sessions is that the transition from storytelling (i.e., external narrative sequences) to emotional differentiation (i.e., internal narrative sequences) was most successful when it was first preceded by a reflexive inquiry mode (see Figure 3.1). Specifically, EFT therapists invite clients to shift from external to reflexive and internal narrative modes to facilitate new emotional meaning making and new perspectives on self and others in the world. In her intensive case analysis of three good outcome and three poor outcome EFT dyads, Lewin (Angus et al., 2004) found that

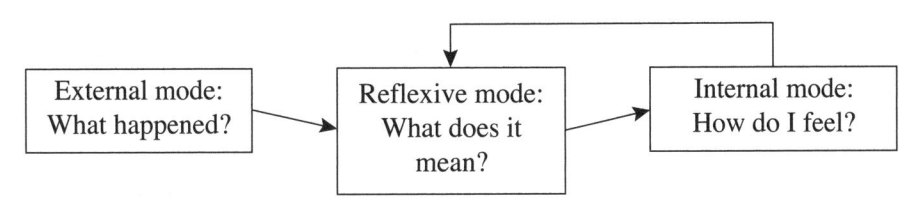

| External mode: What happened? | → | Reflexive mode: What does it mean? | → | Internal mode: How do I feel? |

Figure 3.1. Successful outcome sequence of three narrative modes.

reflexive to internal mode shifts comprised almost a third (30%) of all narrative process mode shifts undertaken by EFT therapists involved in the good outcome therapy relationships. In contrast, poor outcome EFT therapists initiated significantly fewer reflexive to internal mode shifts (16.75%) than their good outcome counterparts. In essence, it appeared as if the EFT therapist's specific focus on emotional meanings, in the context of the client's self-reflections, helped the client to enter more fully into a sustained elaboration of their own internal world of felt emotions as experienced in the therapy session. The client's exploration of intense feelings of vulnerability and emotional pain were also sustained by a sense of safety and trust in the therapist.

A primary goal of EFT task interventions, such as two-chair and empty-chair tasks, is the heightening of client emotional arousal to facilitate shifts in emotional processes. Emotion shifts can be in the form of movement from maladaptive secondary emotions to more primary adaptive emotional responses or the accessing of new adaptive emotional responses in the context of maladaptive emotion schematic memories. Experiencing new, and sometimes contradictory, emotional responses in the context of autobiographical memories can lead to significant shifts in the intentions, hopes, beliefs, wishes, and feelings that are attributed to the actions of self and others. At these moments, we see ourselves and others in a new light and are impelled to construct a new, emotionally coherent narrative that accounts for what happened and why it occurred, what was felt, in relation to whom, and about what need or issue. It is our contention that emotions are "understood" and have personal meaning when organized within a narrative framework that identifies what is felt, about whom, and in relation to what need or issue.

Facilitating Narrative Process Change

Two techniques are particularly helpful for heightening and symbolizing client emotional engagement with significant life stories: (a) facilitating client disclosures of significant relationship events and (b) expressing unresolved feelings and meanings in two-chair and empty-chair dialogues.

Retelling Significant Relationship Events

A growing number of psychotherapy researchers (Elliott, Watson, et al., 2004; Greenberg, Rice, et al., 1993; Greenberg & Safran, 1987; Mahoney, 1991; Pennebaker, 1995) are recognizing the importance of emotional disclosure as a basis for the generation of new meanings of self and others and macronarrative change in psychotherapy. The more evocative and descriptive the client can be in the session regarding his or her experiences, the greater the opportunity the therapist has to empathically resonate with, and attune to, the client's feeling state. We have found the use of metaphor phrases (Angus & Rennie, 1988, 1989) to be particularly productive in deepening client experiencing in sessions and providing a shared imaginal context of understanding between client and therapist. For example, in the American Psychological Association DVD *Narrative Therapy* (2007), Angus demonstrated the facilitation of emotional and narrative processes in an initial therapy session through the introduction of a key metaphor phrase. At an early juncture in the session, after the client had begun to explore her experience of "taking in and taking in everyone's problems," Angus suggested to the client that her experience of being the only person in her family who was able to provide support to her parents had left her feeling like "a container that is so full that it is now sinking under the sheer weight of the burdens being carried." The metaphor phrase seemed to strike a resonant experiential chord for the client who fully elaborated how the recognition of these feelings of being "weighed under" were key to her understanding her own feelings of depression and seeking professional help. The creation of a shared sense of experiential meaning between client and therapist seemed to facilitate an early turning point in the session that allowed the client to more openly explore her recent experiences of depression in the session.

In addition, we have found the strategic use of open-ended, scaffolding questions to be an invaluable tool when engaging clients in productive storytelling, meaning making, and emotional differentiation processes. *Scaffolding questions* are designed to help therapists target key processing markers for further client differentiation during therapy sessions. For instance, a scaffolding question such as "Could you provide me a specific example of that happening in your life?" helps clients shift to the disclosure and narration of specific, image-based personal memories that are more likely to activate experienced emotions and entry into the client's lived experience of important life events. Alternatively, questions such as "So, when he slammed the door and walked out on you, what was happening inside you? It felt as if . . ." help clients to reflect on their emotions. Finally, meaning-making scaffolding questions help clients to reflect on the personal significance of new emotional understandings and narrative disclosures during therapy sessions. Scaffolding questions such as "What does that story say about you?" help clients to reflect on, symbolize, and acknowledge important cherished values and purposes that define who they are and what they stand for in life.

Empty-Chair Task Interventions

Empty-chair dialogue is an example of a role-play intervention that originated in gestalt therapy (Perls et al., 1951) and has been adapted for use in EFT to help clients confront a significant other—in imagination—to transform maladaptive emotions and construct a new, more differentiated and compassionate account of the unresolved situation or unfinished business. In the case of emotional injury, empty-chair interventions are designed to help clients undertake an experiential entry into the internal world or perspective of the significant other with whom they have experienced relationship problems. The process of resolving unfinished business using empty-chair dialogue has been rigorously modeled (Greenberg, Rice, et al., 1993) and empirically verified (Paivio & Greenberg, 1995).

When facilitating this intervention during a therapy session, therapists are encouraged to follow an empathic style and, having established an alliance, introduce an empty-chair dialogue when they detect a marker of unfinished business. Such markers typically involve the client giving expression to lingering unresolved feelings toward a significant other or to statements of painful childhood memories. Interrupted or restricted expressions of anger over past treatment, and/or nonverbal behavior, such as stifling tears or holding one's breath, often accompany these moments in therapy sessions. A vital element in this process of engaging in lively contact with the imagined other is that creative adjustment is facilitated by the restorying of the person's emotional memories and the emergence of new views of self and significant others. Emotional arousal (Greenberg & Korman, 1993) is viewed as a key mechanism in evoking salient memories and accessing self–other schematic structure.

In addition to accessing and expressing painful emotions, addressing the fundamental intentions of the other is key to resolving emotional injuries in EFT. Specifically, clients are seeking answers to the painful question "Why did they hurt me?" The issue of intention goes directly to fundamental issues of trust and attachment and the belief that others are trustworthy and loving. When the actions of loved ones cause us emotional pain, we are often left confused and unable to meaningfully integrate feelings of anger, betrayal, fearfulness, and sadness. Central to the quest for understanding is the construction of a new, emotionally coherent account that integrates the external narrative (i.e., what happened) with a more differentiated and rich account of the internal and reflexive narrative, in which the questions "What do I feel?" and "What does it mean?" are more fully addressed.

The following example of an empty-chair intervention, as cited in Angus and Bouffard (2004), demonstrates the important role that the therapist's expressed empathy, selective questions, and suggestions play in helping the client to engage in internal and reflexive narrative mode in relation to experiences of trauma and loss. The therapist's responses help scaffold (i.e., build) the client's reflexive processing of implicit meanings attendant on the personal memory and help differentiate new emotional responses emerging from her active engagement in her inner experiential world.

In this sequence the therapist first has the client imaginatively place her mother, who committed suicide when the client was an adolescent, in an empty chair and then asks the client to describe the trauma scene, followed by an encouragement to elaborate felt emotions. The client in turn shifts back and forth between describing the remembered suicidal scene and articulating felt emotions evoked by the terrifying images. In this therapeutic dance, the therapist empathically follows the client's lead and facilitates the expression of painful emotions and deep fears. Finally, the client shifts to a reflexive questioning mode at the end of the sequence in an attempt to bring understanding to this trauma experience.

Therapist: Tell her what you remember about the things, about the memories. [Therapist invites specific client narrative disclosure.]

Client: The horror and the terror [becomes tearful]. [Client focuses on felt experience in response to internalized image of mother at the suicide scene.]

Therapist: Let it go. [Therapist stays with the client focus on felt emotions and differentiates fear, horror, and terror.] Tell her about your fear [Client takes a tissue], the horror, and the terror. Stay with it; you're doing well. What do you remember? Tell her what it's like for you. It's important.

Client: [crying] I feel these memories are absolutely horrific and things I never should have seen.

Therapist: Tell her.

Client: It's etched so deeply in my mind, I can't erase it. When I think of you, I can't even think of you because I just remember you.

Therapist: Tell her what you see [Therapist invites disclosure of imaged trauma scene].

Client: All I see is just you lying there. I can't believe it, and you're not waking up.

Therapist: Not waking up. What's it like for you? [Therapist invites a shift to emotional awareness of reexperiencing the trauma scene].

Client: I'm just so afraid [Client emotional disclosure and differentiation].

Therapist: "I feel terrified" [Therapist empathic reflection and emotional differentiation]. That's good. Keep breathing. "I feel terrified." What's going on?

Client: And absolute disbelief. [Client shifts to reflexive mode.] How could you, how could you?

Therapist: So, "How could you do this?" [Therapist invites client to confront his mother directly with his reflexive questions in a search for understanding and meaning.] Tell her this.

Client: I don't really understand why you did it.

Therapist: Stay with those memories, and what do you want to say? What are you feeling now? [Therapist invites client to elaborate felt emotions.]

Client: [Client continues in reflexive narrative mode.] I'm thinking that, um, how can I, how can something that happened so long ago control me so much now.

Two-Chair Task Interventions

Two-chair dialogues are specifically designed to address the harsh self-critical processes that are central to working effectively with depression in EFT (Greenberg & Watson, 2006). With this role-play strategy, the self-critical voice that often dominates a client's self-narrative is placed in one chair and criticizes another aspect of self, and the client then expresses the response of the experiencing self to the harsh self-critic. The objective is to have clients become emotionally self-aware of the painful impact of the critic and, in response, forcefully protest and resist the voice of the critic by expressing core needs for nurturance, support, and validation that have been long diminished and suppressed. Again, therapist empathic attunement to the leading edge of the client's experience during the chair intervention helps facilitate client narrative process shifts from the detailed description of a painful life event (external narrative mode) to self-critical reflection on the behavior (reflexive narrative mode) and a sustained elaboration of the emotional consequences of the critic (internal narrative mode) on the experiencing self. The following two-chair intervention demonstrates this narrative process pattern.

Client: At the department meeting yesterday, my supervisor, Dan, scolded me for not letting him know that we are behind on finalizing the budget estimates for our next conference. I was just so taken aback and upset that I could not say a word. He knows that it is his fault, but all I could do was apologize, again. [Event description/external narrative mode]

Therapist: So, apologizing even though you'd like to stand up. What happens inside you when he's scolding you? [Invites client shift to reflexive mode]

Client: I just heard that old voice again [sighs]: You're a weepy mess who's always giving in.

Therapist: Can you move to the other chair and be that critical voice?

Client: OK.

Therapist: Now can you say it again? "You're a weepy...."

Client: You're a weepy mess that's always giving in. It's never important enough to you; you know you're not important.

Therapist: OK [Client sniffs], come back here. [Client sighs, sniffs, sighs.] How are you feeling here right now? [Invites client shift to emotional differentiation/internal narrative mode.]

Client: It makes me feel lousy.

Therapist: Mm-hmm, just lousy. Can you say that to her? Tell her.

Client: [Sniffs] I feel bad.

Therapist: What's that make you feel like or feel like doing?

Client: I just want to hide. [Primary maladaptive emotion action tendency]

Therapist: Mm-hmm. Kind of ashamed?

Client: Yeah, like I'm a failure.

Therapist: What do you need from her? [Invites client shift to meaning exploration/reflexive narrative mode.]

Client: I, uh, I need more time and support to get myself all together.

Therapist: What do you need from her right now?

Client: I guess I need from her right now to be more emotionally supportive [sniffs], and if you see me weakening and giving in, sort of pull myself up—pull me up—and, sort of, talk to me and say, like, keep calm but don't, don't apologize.

Therapist: Mm-hmm.

Client: You know, you can do it. I'm here with you. You can be strong. We'll do it together.

Therapist: OK, so you want her to say that to you, you want her to say: We can do it together. Be strong. I'm here.

Client: Yes.

Therapist: Can you say that again to her? [Client sniffs.] Exactly what you want?

Client: I need you to be there for me, be supportive.

Therapist: Mm-hmm, and when you start seeing that I'm giving in [*Client:* Mm-hmm.], I'll say, "I'm here. We're together. I'm supporting you, so be strong and don't give in."

Clients' disclosures of personal stories and the subsequent elaboration of action, emotion, and meaning are fundamental to the facilitation of significant personal change in narrative-informed EFT. Findings emerging from the intensive empirical analyses of narrative process shifts in productive EFT sessions indicate that successful therapists explicitly focus on strategies that enable clients to disclose their most important lived experiences as stories such that they can dwell on, and articulate more fully, emotions and new personal meanings. A key strategy includes the differentiation of adaptive emotions, implicit beliefs, hopes, intentions, and expectations of self and others caught up in the unfolding events of the story. Successful EFT therapists actively facilitate clients' disclosures of emotionally salient personal memories (external narrative mode) to enable elaborated reflection (reflexive narrative mode) on emerging emotional experiences (internal narrative mode) for the articulation of new personal meaning and story reconstruction.

CONCLUSION

This chapter has provided a broad overview of narrative-informed EFT. The next chapter explores a critical aspect of this approach. Like traditional (i.e., nonnarrative) EFT, our approach is marker guided. Research has demonstrated that in sessions, EFT clients have specific emotional processing problems that are identifiable by clients' in-session statements and behaviors (Greenberg, Elliott, & Lietaer, 1994; Greenberg, Rice, et al., 1993; Rice & Greenberg, 1984). These problem indicators, or problem markers, indicate underregulated, overregulated, and unintegrated emotions. EFT therapists are trained to identify markers of different types of problems and to intervene in specific ways that best suit these problems. However, unlike traditional EFT, our approach uses narrative problem markers. Chapter 4 identifies common narrative problem markers and corresponding interventions.

4

PROBLEM MARKERS: SAME OLD STORIES, EMPTY STORIES, UNSTORIED EMOTIONS, AND BROKEN STORIES

Identifying client process markers is an important task in narrative-informed EFT because it helps therapists to intervene in different ways and at different points in time to effectively address specific problem subtypes. In this chapter we discuss four key narrative-emotion problem markers and intervention strategies. First, we define markers of *same old story*—repetitive, unproductive experience based on core maladaptive emotion schemes—and explain how best to address these therapeutically. Then we discuss how therapists can best deal with *empty stories*, or clients' autobiographical memory disclosures that are stripped of lived emotional experience. Next, we discuss how clients present undifferentiated affect as unstoried emotions and how therapists can best promote narrative contextualization and regulation of this type of dysregulated emotional states in therapy sessions. Finally, we address how to best deal with *broken stories*, which are states of narrative incoherence in which competing plotlines, and their accompanying emotions, block clients' efforts to achieve an integrated understanding of an emotionally unresolved or traumatic life experience. Narrative problem markers, the differential interventions most suited to each, and the desired in-session outcomes are presented in Table 4.1 and discussed in the remaining sections of this chapter.

Table 4.1
Client Problem Markers and End-States Tasks

Marker	Intervention	End state
1. **Same old story.** An overgeneral description or summary of a repetitive maladaptive theme. (a) A pronounced sense of stuckness and helplessness from repetitive engagement in unrewarding interactions despite negative consequences. (b) Often expressed in a flat external voice, suggesting the narrative is not new. (c) Linguistic indicators such as "never" and "always." (d) Problematic patterns are viewed as being maintained by forces outside of the self; low personal agency.	(a) Get a specific example: an autobiographical memory that exemplifies the same old story. (b) Explore and elaborate feelings and intentions in the context of the story for heightened sense of agency. (c) Identify core maladaptive schemes, scripts, and negative plotlines. Access antidote emotion. Gain agency reauthoring story.	A new plotline with self as agent.
2. **Empty stories.** Stories stripped of expected emotional content. (a) Focus on external details. (b) Minimal experiential engagement with the event. (c) Recounted as if a disengaged bystander. (d) Personal significance of the story is unclear.	(a) Attend to and symbolize process and bodily felt experience and emotion. (b) Evocative empathy to enter into experience. (c) Integrate experience with what happened. (d) Deepen understanding of impact of event.	Emotion informs and moves the construction of new meaning. The client is empowered to have needs met. The client is aware of the significance of what the story means to him or her.

3. **Unstoried emotions.** Expression of a maladaptive emotional state devoid of narrative context or connection to a trigger.
   (a) Dysregulated.
   (b) No discernable cause.
   (c) No relational or situational context identified.
   (d) No understanding of emotion.
   (e) Client feels like a helpless victim of a symptom.

   (a) Contextualize within relational and situational contexts.
   (b) Identify cues that are triggers that evoke emotion.
   (c) Coconstruct coherent story: beginning, middle, and end.
   (d) Move to symbolize primary emotion.
   (e) Externalize symptomatic aspects of experience.

   Integration of emotion and narrative for reflection and new meaning. The client understands the emotional awareness of significance of what it means to him or her.

4. **Broken stories.**
   Emotional incoherence subtype: conflicting emotional plotlines in which competing emotional responses and action tendencies impede resolving problems.
   (a) Confusion, uncertainty, puzzlement, frustration, and protest regarding inability to let go and move on.
   (b) Questioning why.
   Narrative incoherence subtype: fragmented story structure.
   (a) Narrative lacks clear beginning, middle, end.
   (b) Fragmented description of subjective experience.
   (c) Confusion about causes or factors.

   (a) Access primary emotions beyond secondary frustration.
   (b) Differentiate, own, and elaborate competing emotions one at a time.
   (c) Restory past events into a coherent story in the context of new understanding of self and others, needs, intentions, and beliefs.
   (d) Explore each plotline one at a time.

   Heightened self-coherence and story integration.
   Self-narrative reorganization.

   (a) Facilitate narrative elaboration of client-specific memory that addresses gaps in timelines, plotlines, and story outcomes for heightened story coherence.
   (b) Articulate the emotions and intentions of the narrator in the context of the organized story.

   Heightened self-coherence and story integration.
   Self-narrative reorganization.

The shared goal for all of these narrative strategies is to help clients adaptively regulate emotional experiences and construct new understandings that support the implementation of new ways of being in the world and a new self-identity narrative. As one client said of her emotional experience in therapy, "When I came into therapy my feelings were like all different color pieces of string rolled up in a big knot . . . now these pieces are all neatly filed together in a box, according to their colors." This evocative metaphor conveys a new sense of self-coherence and emotional integration that emerged for this client over the course of her therapy experience. Another EFT client poignantly remarked, "It is still a horrific picture, but now I know she loved me and it wasn't my fault," when describing the beneficial impact of expressing profound feelings of anger, fear, and sadness that had been evoked by her mother's suicide. Although the actual events of the story remain intact, the emotional meaning of those actions undergoes a profound change and is the basis for the emergence of a new view of self, present, past, and future.

SAME OLD STORY

We use the term *same old story* to identify when clients disclose overgeneral descriptions of maladaptive interpersonal patterns and emotional states. As indicated in Table 4.1, same old stories have the following features: (a) they evince strong feelings of experiential "stuckness," and repetitions that remain resistant to change despite painful interpersonal consequences and story outcomes; (b) they are often expressed in a flat, external voice that suggests the narrative is not new and has been told on many other occasions; (c) they are marked by linguistic indicators that herald the imminent disclosure of a same old story, including phrases such as "he never" "she always" "once again I am left holding the bag" and "it is always the same; he yells and I hide"; and (d) they convey that the problematic patterns are seen as being maintained by forces outside of the self; thus, there is a low sense of personal agency.

For example, a woman who has been divorced for a number of years repeatedly begins her therapy session with a litany of complaints about her ex-husband. Her anger and resentment convey both her feelings of being victimized by the past actions of her husband and a sense of stuckness in an unsatisfying same old story that has come to define her. One EFT client disclosed the following same old story to her therapist:

> I guess I have just learned to cope with it or just hide my feelings—I have always done that. It's just followed and followed [me], and my mother still hides her feelings until now . . . she'd done it all her life.

A key characteristic of same old stories is that they often represent generalized patterns of actions and emotions rather than specific events, and as such, they tend to be low in imagery, lack specific details as to time or place, and evoke little emotional activation. Finally, as evidenced in the foregoing statement, clients often mention a strong history of the recurrence of the same old story pattern among immediate family members that provides a clue to the developmental origins of the maladaptive pattern and why it may be so difficult to change. These may involve core conflictual relationship themes, such as always feeling rejected and withdrawing, or core self-themes, such as feeling like a failure and feeling helpless.

Same old stories tend to proliferate at the beginning of therapy relationships and can therefore be helpful early indicators of tacit, maladaptive emotion schemes that remain unprocessed and unresolved. The underlying maladaptive schemes influence explicit processes and manifest as same old stories, which indicates that their source will be important to address over the course of treatment. Given that core emotional schemes are not usually available to awareness, they are expressed in the context of clients' same old stories, and their output as same old stories is an important source of clinical information for case formulation and setting treatment tasks and goals.

An intensive case analysis of dyads from the York I Depression Study (Bryntwick, Angus, Boritz, & Greenberg, 2011) indicated that EFT clients who do not fully recover from depression at treatment termination tell significantly more same old stories in early phase, middle phase, and late phase therapy sessions than EFT clients who are not depressed at treatment termination. In essence, it appears that the clients who are still depressed at treatment termination continue to remain stuck in their same old stories across sessions. In contrast, more successful clients first protest and then challenge the core assumptions of their same old stories by undertaking and experiencing new, positive story outcomes.

To help clients adaptively change their same old stories, EFT therapists need to help them to access and disclose emotionally salient, specific autobiographical memories that are higher in imagery and emotional arousal and evoke a reexperiencing, rather than just a retelling, of the personal memory. It is important that the EFT therapist empathically scaffold a client's reentry into the lived experience of the same old story so that a more differentiated account of intentions and feelings can be articulated for further reflection and new meaning making. The goal is to access core maladaptive schemes that generate the scripts and stuck negative plotlines of the clients' stories and to help clients author a new plotline with the self as agent. In this task, core maladaptive emotion schemes need to be activated, articulated in language, reflected on, and transformed to form new explicit narratives that can guide clients' conscious lives. Maladaptive emotion schemes can be activated by attention to the body and/or by recalling specific, autobiographical memory narratives. They can then be understood through reflection on bodily felt experiences that are produced in the context of retelling the story of what happened. The following excerpt from an EFT session evocatively demonstrates this process.

Client: So, once again I have that feeling that I have to give up and recognize that I am outnumbered; there is nothing I can do [same old story] . . . I'm getting the same feeling right now that I used to get when my husband came home—you know—that the stomach tightens up?

Therapist: What feeling is that?

Client: Of "here it comes"; where you got to . . .

Therapist: Brace yourself.

Client: Yeah, brace yourself—you know—for what's going to happen next.

Therapist: Can you tell me about a specific time in which you felt that way?

Identification of clients' core maladaptive emotion schemes in the context of emotionally salient same old stories is also a central aspect of making a case formulation in EFT (Greenberg & Goldman, 2007). The therapist follows the client's pain and unfolds the narrative in which it is embedded to identify the core scheme, which often entails sadness and fear of abandonment or shame associated with feelings of inadequacy. Once identified, the narrative in which the schemes are embedded, such as the shame-based narrative of having been pushed to achieve but never being good enough or the abandonment-based narrative of feeling excluded from the family as the unfavored child, becomes the focus of, and provides the theme of, therapy. Once activated, emotion schemes enable heightened access to emotionally salient autobiographical memory narratives, affective experiences, and nonverbal responses that provide a script for how to be in situations. It is in this manner that clients' disclosures of specific, emotionally salient autobiographical memory narratives in EFT help facilitate emotional and self-identity change in EFT. The following excerpt from an EFT session demonstrates the therapist's use of empathic reflection to highlight a relationally based maladaptive emotion scheme from childhood.

Client: The memories I have preceding age 4, they are always, like, in regards to pleasing people and making them feel good. My mom was working during the day, but in the mornings, and

> she always would bring in this baby bottle for me, and I remember one morning she brought it and I took it and I started sucking. Ooh God, I hate this taste, but somehow I knew it is important for her—you know—like part of her daily routine and also, like, the contact between me and her and the preparations and everything. I couldn't say anything and this is what I do all the time. [Same old story]
>
> *Therapist:* So, it's pretty amazing at 2-and-a-half you were already so attuned that this would hurt her, that I'm going to drink this anyway and not ruin it for her, like, "I sacrifice myself."

In the foregoing example, the therapist's empathic reflection highlights the emotional meaning of the same old story pattern for the client, wherein agentic, caring intentions are identified as motivating the actions of the child rather than simply being a passive acquiescence to the demands of others. In contrast to a same old story from the past, the following therapy session excerpt illustrates the activation of an emotion scheme as a same old story in the context of a client's current life.

> *Client:* It's always the same: I let down my guard and then find out that I have trusted the wrong person and I am afraid that it will happen again. [Same old story] What happens with James is when I see him enter the room I feel emotion towards him—just like different emotions—but up until about a week ago, like, friendship.
>
> *Therapist:* Is that kind of like a feeling of warmth? [Empathic conjecture, differentiating emotional experience and symbolizing]
>
> *Client:* Exactly! I was about to say a trust, a warmth, just this complete contentment. [Symbolizing the synthesized bodily felt sense]
>
> *Therapist:* That feels really good inside.
>
> *Client:* Exactly, and, um, it's followed by this gut-wrenching, sick feeling of dread because the only other person in the last 4 years that has made me feel that way was Stephen and it turned out to be exactly opposite to everything that was really going on, like when I thought he most liked me and most accepted me for who I was, it was a huge act.

In EFT, the therapist essentially follows a two-stage approach of arriving at and then leaving the emotional experience that is embedded in clients' same old stories (Greenberg, 2002). In the first stage, the therapist helps the client to articulate and explore the emotional significance of the client's same old story. For instance, in the foregoing example, the therapist might ensure that the client had fully arrived at her maladaptive emotional experience by focusing back on her activated experience of dread. To further attend to, welcome, symbolize, and explore it, the therapist might say, "Let's stay with this feeling of sickness and dread that just hits you in the gut when you are reminded of Stephen. Can you stay with it and breathe?" This draws the client's attention to the trauma-based emotion memory schemes and the responses associated with them. The client, articulating a belief that helps narrate the experience, might now say, "It's like I can't open up; I'll just be hurt again." It is the quest for knowing and naming what is felt and for knowing what it means or says about one in the context of a specific situation or relationship that heralds the shift to the next level of experiential processing.

Having arrived at a core maladaptive feeling and an articulated sense of its personal meaning, the goal in therapy then shifts to having the client access a more adaptive emotional resource as an antidote to the maladaptive feeling. This shift heralds the movement to the second stage of the EFT intervention. Focusing on the alternate feeling already present in the room, the feeling of "trust, a warmth, just this complete contentment" might do this. If this were not present as the source of an alternate voice, the therapist could access a more adaptive emotional response by helping the client articulate a need, asking, "What do you need in this deep feeling of hurt and distrust?" The client might respond with, "I just need to be held and to be comforted. I do so want some of the warmth." The therapist would then put this more adaptive voice in a dialectical interaction with the voice of dread by saying, "So, what are you saying to the dread and to the voice that says, "I can't open up?" The client might say, "I know I need to go slow to protect myself but I also need to recognize what is different in this relationship." Access to adaptive needs is central in accessing new feelings that undo old feelings (Greenberg, 2002, 2010).

Once new, transformative feelings are accessed, EFT therapists focus on the facilitation of new meaning making and self-identity reconstruction. Client agency needs to be highlighted and clearly symbolized in a new narrative that reauthors the past narrative and sets up new plotlines for the future. Often, new metaphors arise capturing the change, such as "no longer being stuck in the mud," now "having my hand on the rudder," or "no longer being in glass cage."

EMPTY STORIES

We use the term *empty stories* to signify when clients disclose salient, distressing and/or disturbing personal memories that are stripped of emotional activation and/or experiential engagement. These stories often provide (a) a detailed chronicle of the external circumstances of an event with (b) little or no elaboration of the meaning or impact of the story for the client. Rather than narrating their own subjective experiencing of an event, (c) the clients recount their story as if they are a disengaged bystander or observer of what happened, and (d) the significance of the story to them is unclear. For example, a client may talk about her recent experience of her husband declaring he wanted a divorce, an eventuality that she had been trying her utmost to stave off. She talks about it in a factual manner referring to the mediation proceedings and child care, without any reference to her sense of hurt, fear, and anger at the injustice of it all.

In turn, the lack of emotional expression in empty stories makes it challenging for EFT therapists to understand what the point of the story is for the client and to develop empathic attunement to the client's lived experience of the event. This may impede the development of a secure emotional bond with the therapist and undermine the client's reflective engagement with the lived experience of the event for the differentiation of new emotional meanings and self-understandings.

Intervention addressing empty stories involves guiding clients inward to symbolize and process the lived experience of a story, rather than a disengaged chronicle of the circumstances of what happened. Evocative empathy and focusing interventions are both used to engage a fuller bodily felt awareness of the emotional impact of the story—especially adaptive emotions—and help clients to articulate the personal significance of the event. When the subjective experiencing of an event can be coherently integrated with the circumstances of what happened, clients are able to deepen their understanding of the impact of the event. Moreover, the activation and articulation of adaptive emotions help clients to take actions in the world to satisfy unmet interpersonal needs and achieve new story outcomes. This excerpt from an EFT session provides an example of an empty story in which a client recounts the disturbing details of an unexpected encounter with a friend:

> They had slept over at our house with their kids, which was not uncommon. You know—we put the kids all to bed so we could stay up all night and talk and stuff. And, uh, for some reason or other, my husband and [the friend's] wife had left. I'm still trying to think of how that situation arose, but it did, and, uh, then this fellow came upstairs, partly dressed. We both knew what it was about. And he kind of looked at me. So, I'm shaking my head, which he had taken for an answer.

In the foregoing excerpt, the client's deep feelings of fear, shame, and confusion that were evoked during the incident in her bedroom are absent from her initial telling of the story to her therapist. Because the story disclosure lacks emotional contextualization, it is unclear how the client actually experienced the event: Was it threatening or playful, disturbing, or amusing? Anticipated or a complete surprise? Her therapist's exploratory empathic inquiry, "And as he looked at you, what was happening inside you?" shifted the client's focus to her own lived experience of the remembered event and enabled her to experientially access and articulate, for the first time, the disturbing feelings of fear and shame that she experienced in response to her friend's actions that night.

When working with clients' empty stories, the key therapist task is to help them integrate the lived experience of salient life events with the circumstances of "what happened" in order to enable new emotional meanings to emerge that enrich and sometimes change key understandings of self and others. EFT therapists model approaching and valuing of emotion in client stories by attuning to the emotionally poignant experience expressed in client stories. By making empathically evocative responses to clients' stories, clients' attention is pointed toward the emotional poignancy of their experiences as an aid to further integrate story and emotion.

Therapists use language carefully in this process, avoiding theoretical talk or external narrative and instead making empathic conjectures that employ the language of clients' internal worlds, describing particular, not general, experiences in sensory, not conceptual, terms. Over time clients learn to attend inwardly, and their awareness of the emotional significance in their experience grows. If emotional experience is blocked, attending inwardly may also require gaining more awareness of the bodily felt experience connected to emotion. The following excerpt demonstrates how empathic exploration and conjectures help a client to emotionally enter her empty story during a therapy session.

Client: They don't particularly want to go anywhere with me; my son wouldn't go shopping with me since he was 10. These boys don't shop with their mothers. So, we couldn't even look for clothes together. I have to give him the money and he goes. The only way I can get them to spend any time is if I offer to take them out for a very expensive dinner.

Therapist: So, this must be very, very painful; you're still wanting that kind of connection with them. You haven't given up on that, and it keeps hurting inside.

Client: We haven't taken a holiday in 3 years. We haven't gone to the show for years. I drive them to the shows and all. Um, they, because of the situation, they've involved themselves with their friends to an extreme.

Therapist: So I hear, "Yeah, yeah, yeah," and I hear more and more examples of the same thing. I have a sense that there's lot of pain underneath what you're telling me.

Client: Yes [tearfully], and it just rips me apart to feel that I just don't matter to them anymore.

In this excerpt, the therapist evocatively captures the underlying pain and sadness—primary adaptive emotions—that underlie the detailed event that the client bitterly expresses during her therapy session. Once we know what we feel, we reconnect to the needs that are being signaled by emotion, and we are motivated to meet our needs. Increased emotional awareness of feelings is therapeutic in a variety of ways. Having accepted the emotions rather than avoiding them, the therapist then helps the client to utilize emotion. What is the information and action tendency in each of the emotions? In the sadness that lasts, what is the loss, and what is the need? In shame, is it a loss of face, of esteem, of position or status, and is the need for comfort and validation, for support, for reconciliation? In the anger, what is the unfairness or frustration; what does one want to do? Is it a violation of one's sense of self, safety, or trust, or was one robbed of something precious? In pain, what is it that is shattered? Is it the sense of self or the bond that one wishes to be whole again? What is the need: self-repair or relationship repair? Here the client learns how to utilize the emotion of which they have become aware and have accepted to improve coping. Clients are helped to make sense of what their emotion is telling them and to identify the goal or need or concern that it is organizing them to attain. Emotion is thus used both to inform and to move.

UNSTORIED EMOTIONS

It is clear that helping clients to tolerate and regulate emotional experience is an important therapist task in EFT. As noted earlier, emotional arousal and expression are not always helpful or appropriate in therapy or in life and, for some clients, must be preceded or accompanied by the development of the capacity for emotional regulation. Any benefits believed to accrue from the intense expression of emotion are generally predicated on the client's prior overregulation (overcontrol)—emotional avoidance or suppression—but it is apparent that for some individuals, and some psychological disorders, emotions are undercontrolled or undifferentiated (Gross, 2002; Linehan, 1993). Important issues in any treatment, then, are what emotions are to be regulated and how they are to be regulated. Generally speaking, underregulated emotions that require down-regulation are usually either secondary emotions, such as despair and hopelessness, or primary maladaptive emotions, such as the shame of being worthless, the anxiety of basic insecurity, and panic (Greenberg, 2002).

We use the term *unstoried emotions* to identify the client's expression of undifferentiated, maladaptive emotional states not embedded in a narrative context. Features of markers of unstoried emotional states include (a) dysregulated emotional states, (b) inability to identify a specific cause or starting point that explains the onset of the emotional response, (c) no relational or situational context, (d) little or no understanding of what the emotional state means to them, or (e) symptomatic reactions. Examples of unstoried emotions are maladaptive states such as paralyzing anxiety, overwhelming sadness and vulnerable fragility, and statements such as "I don't know why, but I have been feeling just so depressed all this week," "I don't understand it: I feel like I just want to fire the world and tell everyone to screw off," or "I am so anxious and stressed that I can't focus on my work. I think I must be going crazy; there just is no reason for it." Although clients will often express deep discomfort regarding experiencing unstoried emotional states (e.g., "I am so overwhelmed by this feeling," "I feel like I am going crazy"), they also feel helpless and powerless to change them. It is as if the emotion is in charge rather than that they are experiencing a situated discrete emotion. It is only when these unexplained emotional states are embedded within a specific narrative context through autobiographical memory recall or engagement in role-play task dialogues that a client can achieve a nuanced understanding of what the feeling specifically means and says about him or her.

Intervention involves further narrative contextualization through personal narrative disclosures or role-play for heightened emotional regulation and new meaning making during therapy sessions. The therapist first helps the client to identify the specific cues that trigger the overwhelming emotional states. Next, through empathic responding, the therapist helps the client to coconstruct a coherent narrative that will now have a clear beginning, middle, and end that organize the events of what happened as an unfolding plotline. Perhaps most important, the narrative contextualization of specific evoking cues helps the client to organize and bring meaning to dysregulated emotional states. Primary emotions, both maladaptive and adaptive, can now be symbolized, and needs can be identified for new meaning creation and goal-oriented actions. Ideally, the client ends this process with a personal story that now integrates emotion and narrative that helps him or her understand the full significance of what happened.

In one example of an unstoried emotion, the distressed client tells her EFT therapist, "I just feel like I have fallen apart inside; I feel so overwhelmed by everything and I am afraid that I am losing my grip again." In the context of exploring what happened in her life over the past week, the EFT therapist was able to help the client discover a connection between the sudden onset of her overwhelming feelings of vulnerability and the unexpected sighting of her ex-husband at a local bar. The narrative contextualization of her unexplained emotion state is the starting point for a number of productive therapeutic outcomes. First, she can now connect her sense of fragility and vulnerability with a specific relational context (i.e., her ex-husband) that conveys important new emotional meanings about self in relation to other. Second, the narrative and relational contextualizations of the emotional state help identify a beginning point or cause for the onset of her distressing feelings that makes the experience more controllable, understandable, and less frightening.

In addition, the EFT therapist's empathic attunement to previously avoided emotions and their associated maladaptive beliefs makes it more likely that the client will experience a shift from feeling stuck in maladaptive primary and secondary emotions to experiencing an agentic engagement with adaptive primary emotions and action tendencies. Finally, like any well-formed narrative, the specification of an experiential beginning point also means that an ending point cannot be too far off, offering the hope of escaping the feeling of being stuck in her negative emotional experience. For the client, there is now a reason for her feelings that convey important information about herself and her ex-husband, which enhances a sense of control and personal agency that undercuts the experiential stuckness of an undifferentiated emotional state.

The following dialogue shows another example of an unstoried emotion. In this example, the therapist helps a client identify the relational context that is evoking new feelings of overwhelming sadness.

Client: I, I, don't really know. I just felt sad and I'm not sure why. Hmm, I mean nothing apparent happened. I don't know, but I was feeling very sad. [Unstoried emotion.]

Therapist: It's hard for you, eh, when you have these feelings of sadness and you don't know where they're coming and . . .

Client: It is hard because . . .

Therapist: And they come over you and you don't know what's going on and you don't understand.

Client: Well, I'm troubled because I don't know where it's coming from; like, I don't understand it and I don't know why I felt so sad. I mean, I, I, I felt sad. I wouldn't say it was depressed or even not happy, I just felt sad.

The therapist's empathic validation of the client's current state of puzzlement and distress sets the stage for the client's further exploration of the impact of "unstoried sadness" on her relationships with others and why it is important to further understand and experience those feelings. Having identified key markers of unstoried emotion and the importance to the client of understanding what they mean, the EFT therapist focuses her inquiry on helping the client to further differentiate and contextualize the poignant sense of acute sadness that she is experiencing during the session that is not connected to current interpersonal situations or relationship events.

Therapist: Sad, as in some sense of aloneness? Something missing? A loss?

Client: Something missing maybe, a little alone. Although I wasn't alone—there was all kinds of people around me at dinner on Sunday night—yeah, just sort of, yeah, sort of lonely and isolated and not quite with the program—you know [laughs]—sort of left out, and—you know—there were moments that night that I remember feeling that I missed my mom not being with us; I felt her absence.

However, EFT therapists can also use role-play interventions to help clients embed undifferentiated emotional states—unstoried emotions—in specific, relational contexts during therapy sessions. As is more fully elaborated in the case example of Alex in Chapter 6, EFT empty-chair interventions presume the identification of a specific relational focus for the differentiation of troubling emotional states. As such, we believe that helping clients to relationally contextualize and then differentiate unstoried emotional states may be a particularly important emotion regulation strategy for clients who have experienced significant emotional trauma in their past.

Finally, another form of unstoried emotion arises when a person experiences a debilitating psychological symptom or emotional state as an event that is somehow happening to them, outside of their voluntary control, such as when clients say, "My panic overtakes me" or "Depression ruins my life or my day." Some clients also see and experience themselves as helpless victims caught in the grip of an addiction or a temper outburst. In all these cases, people experience themselves as passive recipients of the symptom, which they feel controls them. When clients indicate that they are feeling like a passive victim of a dysregulated emotional or maladaptive behavioral pattern, it can be helpful for the therapist to symbolize the behavior or emotion as an unhelpful agentic external force that endows the client with counteragency, to protest its influence and work against it. This type of externalizing intervention was made popular by Michael White (2004) in his famous treatment of "sneaky poo," in which the symptom of soiling the bed (i.e., the sneaky poo) was made into an agent separate from the child that could be dealt with as an intrusive, unwanted experience. To facilitate the mobilization of the client's agency to counteract the influence of the problematic emotion or behavior, a skilled EFT therapist might ask, "What do you want to say to the panic?" or "How does the panic take you over?" Alternatively, an EFT therapist, in the context of an empty-chair roleplay, might invite the client to become the panic and experientially overtake the client in the imagined role-play.

BROKEN STORIES

The term *broken stories* is used to represent narrative description of emotionally salient life events and interpersonal interactions in which there is a clash between two competing plotlines: the expected, or hoped for, and the emerging, or actual, plotline. So, this marker represents those in-session situations in which clients are struggling to come to terms with competing or troubling emotions, having experienced a disruption of the trajectory of a cherished plotline. Now there is a clash between two competing plotlines: the previously dominant expected or hoped for plotline and the emerging or actual plotline. The client finds the disruption painful and experiences puzzlement or confusion in relation to the discrepancy between anticipated and actual outcomes. Trauma shatters existing plotlines. The experience of a disrupted life narrative can result in one of two possible types of broken story. First, the client may experience a sense of *emotional incoherence*, a confusing array of contradictory feelings that are experienced in relation to an important life concern. Second, it may be that the actual narrative of a life story cannot be told in a coherent fashion because of the disruptive interruption of painful emotions that are evoked in the context of remembering a distressing or traumatic life event. Hence, the two subcategories of broken stories are discussed next: emotional incoherence and narrative incoherence.

Emotional Incoherence

In our work with EFT clients, the most common subtype of markers of a broken story addresses a sense of emotional incoherence in which there is an experience of the disruption of a narrative trajectory that sets up competing, contradictory emotional plotlines (e.g., sadness and anger), and this results in feelings of confusion, stuckness, and self-incoherence (e.g., "Why is it like this?" or "How do I make sense of this?").

This marker includes the following features: (a) A dominant narrative plotline is shattered by actual or feared events; (b) there is a breach of cherished beliefs in relation to what was anticipated or expected and/or basic sense of security or stability in the world; (c) there is a struggle, a questioning (e.g., "Why?" "I'm wondering," "I'm confused"), and a protest regarding inability to let go and move on; and (d) there is client puzzlement and confusion regarding the relentless hold of past troubling memories (e.g., "I thought I had done with my past, but it appears that my past is not done with me").

Life's traumas and major losses or disappointments leave people with a shattered sense of self and world. Cherished beliefs about what is, what will be, or what ought to have been are shattered; one is left with a story one does not want to have, and yet the old story, which provided coherence and security, is no more. For example, one client came into therapy for help in how to deal with having recently received a diagnosis of a child's future long-term disability. Not only was there the loss of the promise of a healthy future adult child but there also was the dilemma of whether to, when to, and how to disclose this to the child.

In the case of emotionally traumatizing personal memories, overpowering, and often contradictory, emotions interfere with the narrator's attempts to organize the experience as a coherent narrative that can be subsequently shared with others and reflected on for further self-understanding. In contrast to unstoried emotions, however, in these broken stories the client is aware of the relational context for the broken story. What remains problematic and is definitive of this broken story emotion incoherence subtype is the presence of deeply competing emotional plotlines, such as shame and sadness at what is lost but anger about life's unfairness or the violation of one's cherished belief. This creates a sense of incoherence for clients about what the story "means" for them and, in the case of trauma and loss, why it happened to them. It is in this way that traumatic memories of loss resist assimilation to preexisting views of self and others in the world. Not surprisingly, childhood experiences of early separation, abandonment, trauma, abuse, and loss are often associated with emotionally incoherent broken stories in adult life, as are adult stories of divorce, betrayal, death of a loved one, and major life failures.

The following therapy session excerpt provides a good example of a client marker of emotional incoherence and demonstrates a number of aspects of this marker that typify this broken story subtype.

Client: It's, like, I have three healthy children, a house. We're not wealthy by any means, but we're okay; um, and I sort of go, "Oh, why am I not happier?" I don't know.

Therapist: Sounds almost like you're saying, "What's the matter with me? What's wrong with me?"

Client: Yes: "What more do I need?"—um—"Am I grateful?" It's funny because you start to feel that you should be grateful but you, you really can't feel grateful. Isn't that awful? That's horrible. It's an awful feeling, you know?

The client is clearly puzzled by and distraught over her unhappiness and believes her feelings are unjustified in the context of an "objective" assessment of her life circumstances, stating, "You start to feel that you should be grateful but you, you really can't feel grateful. Isn't that awful? That's horrible." However, the client is aware of the discrepancy between her "expected" and actual emotional responses that she experiences in relation to her family life.

There are a number of important ways in which EFT therapists can help clients articulate more emotionally coherent personal stories, which help create new perspectives on self and identity reconstruction. Therapists can help by

- accessing, heightening, expressing primary adaptive emotions and action tendencies beyond the secondary frustration and puzzlement;
- facilitating the owning, elaborating, and differentiating of competing emotions and plotlines; accepting the new plotline;
- restorying past events in the context of new self-understanding generated by accessing primary feelings and needs and cherished beliefs not previously acknowledged;
- articulating new understandings of how the story is important to the client now and in the future; and
- enhancing story integration, self-coherence, new and self-narrative reconstruction and reorganization.

For example, building from the client's emerging awareness of the discrepancy between her "expected" and actual emotional responses that she experiences in relation to her family life, her therapist might say something such as,

> It is just so puzzling and almost disturbing to find yourself feeling unhappy and perhaps almost sad in the midst of a life that you always thought would bring you happiness . . . that somehow your feelings about your life right now are totally at odds with what you anticipated would happen and leave you wondering if there is something wrong with you. I wonder if it might be important for us to explore more fully just where those feelings of unhappiness come from—what part of your life that they are connected to—so we can understand more fully how they fit into your life right now.

This invitation for meaning exploration would perhaps validate the client's experience of feeling unhappy in her current life and provide a context for inquiry to access, symbolize, and story those emotions for new meaning making and self-integration.

In a recent intensive case analysis of emotion narrative subtypes, Bryntwick et al. (2011) found that EFT clients who recover from depression start to experience a variety of emotional reactions in relation to their most essential personal stories and life concerns. The narrative expression of two or more possible emotional plotlines in the context of a salient life event can result in a profound sense of experiential incoherence that leaves a client unable to take action to resolve the situation and make meaning of what has happened. To address this sense of emotional incoherence, effective EFT therapists first help clients to symbolize and differentiate each emotional plotline and then purposefully help the client to elaborate and highlight one self-state so that the client, in response, could assertively express the concerns and emotions of the other. The elaboration of two competing emotional plotlines—and the hopes, intentions, desires, and action tendencies they evoke—sets the stage for an open dialogue between different self-positions and the possibility of coconstructing a new, more integrative understanding that enhances a sense of self-coherence and agency. In the following example, a depressed client and her EFT therapist coarticulate in the therapy session the competing sides or "voices" of her emotional incoherence. The client expresses a newly emerging feeling of resentment toward her mother in which she wants her mother to pay for past wrongs, in contrast to a previously expressed narrative of forgiveness and acceptance.

Client: This is the first time I've ever experienced—you know—to let it . . .

Therapist: You've never said she should have . . .

Client: Well, in my mind or to myself, but not to anybody else, maybe I used to think it wasn't—you know—something really important.

Therapist: Yeah, so now just saying them somehow is a relief.

Client: Yeah, it feels good to get that out, it does. It's like I said, the other voice that tells me—you know—she's got to pay some more or—you know—she did that, and it's like she doesn't really deserve to have a relationship with me.

Therapist: Like she doesn't deserve to have me in her life or . . .

Client: Yeah, something like that.

Therapist: So there's this part of you that really feels that strong resentment towards her.

Client: Yeah, yeah, and then the other part wants to just—you know—forgive and carry on.

Therapist: Mm-hmm, so those are likely conflicting forces within you—right—like, almost two complete discrepant voices that one's saying, "No, no, no, she should pay."

Client: Yeah, and the other is like—you know—"Forgive; she's your mother and she's human. She makes mistakes too." I feel like I'm caught, like a yo-yo [laughs].

This excerpt is an excellent example of a broken story. The client conveys that she has not previously shared this experience with anyone when she states, "This is the first time I've ever experienced—you know—to let it . . . Well, in my mind or to myself, but not to anybody else." She seems to have deemed it trivial but then experiences relief after it is expressed: "It feels good to get that out." Therapist ("So there's this part of you that really feels that strong resentment towards her") and client, ("And then the other part wants to just—you know—forgive and carry on") took turns contributing pieces to this broken story such that it emerged richly elaborated. As discussed in Chapter 3, two-chair and empty-chair interventions can help clients to elaborate, differentiate, and dialogue with competing emotional plotlines for the ultimate activation of primary adaptive emotional responses, needs, and action tendencies. Specifically, the activation of primary emotional action tendencies helps clients to access their most fundamental goals and needs that shape future actions, intentions, and behaviors and, where possible, instantiate a new, more agentic experience and view of self.

In contrast, clients who remained depressed over the course of treatment seemed to remain unaware of their puzzling or unusually negative reactions to certain situations or did not communicate awareness that they were portraying mixed emotions. In the excerpt that follows, a client spoke of his relationship to his mother, whom he perceived to be unloving. Although deeply wounded by her, the client could not express his pain. In addition, he believed his mother to be unaware of the damage she had caused him. In this example from a session toward the end of therapy, the therapist articulated the client's predicament in an effort to move the stalled therapy along.

Client: I don't think too many people realize how uncomfortable and how virtually destroying it is, because I think, um, it's very injurious to my self-respect to have such rejection by my mother.

Therapist: I guess in a way you're saying that—you know—it would be very hard; I mean—you know—as you say, she doesn't know the pain you're in; the only way that she would know was if you'd expressed it, but somehow for you, expressing that pain in some way leaves you vulnerable [*Client:* Yes.], so there's the dilemma: I'm afraid I'm going to be rejected, it's very hard for me to open up like this and expose myself in the first place, and then the fear of being rejected—not being recognized—would be just be too humiliating, and yet how else is she going to know what I'm feeling.

Here the therapist attempts to articulate the broken story by symbolizing the disruption of the hoped-for responsive mother who would listen to the client's pain and know what he is feeling and the reality of the feared rejection and humiliation he knows he will get. He cannot recreate the competing plotlines of the wished-for, responsive, and the actual, rejecting, mother. The client then confirms the validity of this broken story but was not an active participant in its expression. As previously mentioned, the client's own awareness and expression of puzzling reactions or competing emotional responses that might facilitate his readiness for therapeutic change were absent. Bryntwick et al. (2011) established in the intensive case analyses that recovered clients articulated more than twice as many broken stories as nonrecovered clients.

Narrative Incoherence

Narrative incoherence means that there are fragmented, unclear, or hard-to-understand stories during which the client appears to be struggling to make sense of, and articulate, an experience. The clients sometimes confess that they are baffled about gaps in their memory of the event or cannot make sense of how the story unfolded. In contrast to unstoried emotions, the clients are aware of the relational context for their broken stories. Process indicators of broken stories that met criteria for narrative incoherence subtype include (a) a lack of a clear sense of the beginning, middle, and end of the story; (b) fragmented descriptions of the internal subjective experiences of protagonists and antagonists; and (c) minimal understanding of causes or factors that contributed to competing emotions, actions, and intentions of self and others in an interpersonal relationship. In addition, narrative incoherence often includes the client's expression of puzzlement about the contents of the story in which they struggle to clearly articulate the circumstances and unfolding events that happened in the story. Not surprisingly, the therapist listening to the story will also find it difficult to understand.

The following example of narrative incoherence occurred during a late-phase therapy session of a poor outcome therapy dyad, drawn from the York I Depression Study. The client was attempting to determine the origin of her cyclical depressive episodes.

Client: Like, I don't think that that's really where my feelings are coming from.

Therapist: I'm not sure what you're saying. You think that something else is responsible for this feeling of depression?

Client: I think that, uh, how I feel about the kids or how I feel about this situation—that is simply a fact. But I don't think that that fact is responsible for my not, um, not some of the things I guess I should be doing or not feeling how I should be feeling. I really find myself just wanting to be alone all the time because, uh—I'm not sure what it's because of.

Therapist: Yeah, I hear you saying—you know—you don't have the energy or the interest in providing [your kids] with other, um, experiences and enriching their lives in other ways. I guess what's missing for me is a sense of what about the sense of

	yourself? There seems to be no interest in giving yourself things, let alone them.
Client:	No, that I don't know why that I don't know why. That bothers me.
Therapist:	So that it is this way is bothersome and confusing as to why, but it is somehow . . .
Client:	Yeah it, it is that way. It is that way but I don't know why. I don't think it is; it is just the kids. I think that's, that's because of me, not, not so much just . . .
Therapist:	It's because of something in you, or something way back.

In the preceding example, the client appears to be perplexed about the origin of her depressed feelings when she states, "I really find myself just wanting to be alone all the time because, uh, I'm not sure what it's because of," and cannot articulate a coherent story about how or why they emerged or what she was truly feeling. In addition, the client's own sense of narrative incoherence seems to affect the therapist, who appears to have difficulty tracking the client at this moment and has to make a number of inferences about, and seek clarification for, her statements.

Effective EFT therapist intervention strategies help clients to recall, experientially enter, and explore the problematic interpersonal event for the identification of new information that addresses key gaps in their recollection for the construction of a coherent story. Specifically, narrative gaps are filled to achieve a clear sense of what happened, of what people felt, and of what it means.

CONCLUSION

A number of narrative-emotion problem markers and the type of interventions helpful at these points have been delineated in this chapter. Indicators of the different markers of same old story, empty stories, unstoried emotion, and broken story have been specified. Together, the markers and preferred interventions constitute therapeutic tasks to help promote new meaning creation in ways relevant to the different markers. In Chapter 5, we delineate emergent meaning markers, which indicate opportunities for capturing and amplifying changes that have already occurred or are in the process of happening. A detailed case example of how EFT therapists effectively work with client narrative incoherence and integrating broken stories is also addressed in further detail in Chapter 5.

5

MEANING-MAKING MARKERS: UNTOLD STORIES, UNIQUE OUTCOME STORIES, AND HEALING STORIES

Three emergent meaning-making markers—untold stories, unique outcome stories, and healing stories—have also been identified in effective emotion-focused therapy (EFT) practice. Each of these narrative-emotion markers provides an opportunity to capture and amplify changes that have already occurred or are in the process of happening. Unlike problem markers, meaning-making markers indicate a new development in the client's self-story that requires therapist intervention for further integration and narrative reconstruction. Table 5.1 summarizes these markers and effective therapist intervention strategies for the facilitation of positive client outcomes.

UNTOLD STORIES

The marker *untold stories* indicates when a client is reexperiencing an emotionally salient personal memory that (a) he or she finds too painful or embarrassing to share with the therapist or (b) is judged to be "unimportant" by the client for disclosure to the therapist. Disclosing untold stories is important because it increases the likelihood that new views of self, self-experiences,

Table 5.1
Emergent Meaning Markers

Marker	Intervention	End state
1. **Untold stories.** Emotionally salient personal experiences that clients have not yet externalized as told stories. The experience (a) appears too painful or embarrassing to share with the therapist or (b) is judged to be "unimportant" by the client for disclosure to the therapist.	(a) Invite client disclosure through evocative, empathic reflections. (b) Facilitate externalization of an internal experience. (c) Probe for an autobiographical memory.	Externalization of salient life experiences as told stories for increased emotion and narrative integration and new meaning making.
2. **Unique outcome stories.** Client expressions of surprise, excitement, contentment, or inner peace that are experienced in relation to comparisons with past maladaptive behaviors. Emotional responses or thought patterns with new, positive intrapersonal and interpersonal outcomes. **Unexpected outcome stories:** A personal story about a surprising event or outcome that documents positive change. (a) Client notices encouraging differences in their own behavior or psychological and emotional well-being, or such differences may be brought to their attention by a significant other (or by significant others).	(a) Notice and heighten client experiences of positive difference and change. (b) Elaborate and amplify what happened and client's contributions and agency.	Heightened awareness and integration of strengths and life possibilities.

82 WORKING WITH NARRATIVE IN EMOTION-FOCUSED THERAPY

- (b) Articulation of a new sense or experience of self in the world.
- (c) Linguistic indicators, including comparisons between past and present behavior, emotional responses of surprise or delight, or thought patterns.
- (d) Expression of surprise, excitement, contentment, or inner peace.

Self-identity change stories: Description of a positive transformation in the overall narrative plotline of their life story and view of self.

- (a) Emergence of new views of self.
- (b) Reconceptualization and identity transformation.

   - (a) Facilitate thematic integration of new view of self in the unique outcome stories.
   - (b) Explore the significance of the new view of self for future life choices and possibilities.

Heightened awareness and integration of strengths and life possibilities.

3. **Healing stories.**
The recollection of a vivid personal memory in which an important relational need was met by a significant other.
- (a) A specific event memory that contains positive emotions such as warmth, security, love, and validation.

   - (a) Focus on newly accessed memory of the unexpected experience of having been cared for by a significant other.
   - (b) Heighten felt experience of receiving that care.
   - (c) Elaborate positive meaning of that experience to restructure the narrative.

Heightened differentiation and integration of connection and validation of lovableness and confidence in interpersonal responsiveness to needs. Restorying.

MEANING-MAKING MARKERS   83

and ways of relating to others will be remembered and transferred to a range of interpersonal contexts and domains in the future (Singer & Salovey, 1993). The process of creating the story also creates an autobiographical memory (ABM) structure that will contain the gist of the story for the rest of one's life. Telling a story is not simply a rehearsal or redescription of a lived experience but an interpersonal act of creation that is, in turn, a memorable relational experience. Therefore, a client's disclosure of emotionally salient life experiences in therapy sessions is both an act of personal memory (re)construction and the creation of a new relational experience with the therapist.

To facilitate client disclosure of salient personal memories, therapists' empathic attunement and evocative reflections often help clients access, externalize, and narrate specific ABMs during therapy sessions. Therapists also need to probe for ABMs at these markers of untold stories. Clients then use the description of vivid ABMs to tell their stories to therapists and to be more fully understood. Explicating untold stories facilitates the development of a strong, trusting therapeutic bond in which both client and therapist cocreate a sense of shared experiencing, knowing, and interpersonal understanding. The therapist's capacity to empathically attend to a client's key concerns, as conveyed in previously untold personal stories, contributes to the early development of a strong, secure therapeutic alliance by instilling a sense of basic trust in the client toward the therapist. In addition, therapists are able to discern problematic interpersonal patterns and maladaptive emotion schemes through both the manner and content of clients' ABM narrative disclosures in untold stories. The outcome of the process of the externalization of salient life experience as told stories is increased emotion narrative integration and new meaning making.

Client statements such as "I don't know if this is important," "For some reason I was just thinking about the summer that my mom died," "I am not sure if it is important to return to all of that stuff that happened," and "It's kind of strange, but I seem to be thinking about my ex-wife a lot these days but I just don't know why" are often indicators that a key emotional concern, intertwined with a series of ABM narratives, is emerging for the client. These appear to be emotionally salient experiences that are either too painful to go into or are judged to be so unimportant that the client would skip over them if not encouraged to unpack them.

The following example, drawn from a good outcome therapy dyad, illustrates how the EFT therapist helps the client to access and disclose salient personal memories,

> Client: And [external narrative shift] especially in the spring—in around May of this year—I was really, um, thinking—the memories were flooding back from 20 years ago in the

Client: spring when I, I left home, and I first discovered I was pregnant.

Therapist: I see.

Client: Really, the weather, the weather in the springtime of this year brought back memories of what happened in May and April of '87.

Therapist: Oh, I see, uh-huh. Is there anything about it that you can sort of recapture and tell me? [*Client:* Uh.] What specific kinds of memories came back?

Client: I just remember pulling together—hastily pulling together—that wedding and all the running around we did to pull it together in 2 weeks.

In another example, the therapist probes for the disclosure of a specific ABM narrative.

Therapist: Uh-huh. So, see if any specific memory comes up of any, of a time when you really felt . . .

Client: Uh, oh yes. [*Therapist:* Uh-huh.] I took, I remember the time when I called home. I called, I called my mother's home just to hear whomever's voice answered. I did it four or five times, and then I would just hang up. [*Therapist:* Hmm.] Just to hear [her family name], just to get in touch with that house that seemed so far away and gone and lost.

The client responds to the therapist's request for a memory by explicating the untold story with a narrative that conveys the sense of the client's poignant longing for the family that she had to leave behind—that she "lost"—when she chose to leave home as a teenager to live with the father of her newborn baby. It is clear that in all of these examples the therapist is actively encouraging the client to shift to the recollection of emotionally significant personal memories and to describe these experiences.

The following example, drawn from another good outcome psychotherapy dyad, illustrates the critical importance of therapist encouragement to explicate an untold story for (a) a client's disclosure and emotional differentiation of a painful past memory and (b) experiential reentry into the lived event for new emotional differentiation and personal meaning reconstruction.

Client: I don't know whether it is good to go back like this or not, is it?

Therapist: I think it is, because it sounds like you're still holding feelings from back then.

Client: If I could just let go of some of these feelings, I think I would be an awful lot happier.

With this interchange, the client, Margaret, seeks out and receives reassurance from her therapist that (a) returning to memories of the past is of key importance for understanding where her problematic emotions "come from" and (b) her feelings of resentment and anger toward her husband are important and point to a personally salient experience that has not yet been fully storied or understood. In pursuit of her goal, she recalls the point at which she first started to feel tensions in her marriage and a growing estrangement from her husband—"the year when everything seemed to happen." In the context of a secure alliance with her therapist, she then discloses a series of emotionally distressing memories involving her disabled parents that happened during "that year."

Client: And I was in the apartment when it was happening [sniffs], and she was telling them that I was forcing her to do this—that sort of thing. And then I went in the elevator to try and bring her back upstairs again. She hit me, and [crying] I think that was the most horrible thing—you know—to stand there in that elevator and your mother hits you, at my age.

Once events have been externalized as a story, clients are able to "stand back" from and actively reflect on their inner world of emotions, intentions, motives, goals, expectations, and beliefs for the identification of effective problem-solving strategies and the construction of more coherent and empowering personal meanings. One good outcome EFT client commented, realizing the full emotional meaning of a previously undisclosed story can be profound:

Um, but sort of having verbalized to you some of those events of the past, it came to me really that, um, there was a great deal of antagonism toward my parents, a lot deeper perhaps than I had thought that it was there. It's something that I have basically suppressed for a very long time.

UNIQUE OUTCOME STORIES

Although a range of cultural themes exist within any given society, many of the culturally inherited stories that we use are "constrictive and blaming" (White, 2007) when it comes to providing a personal account of a troubling life experience or interpersonal relationship. Self-identity narratives often omit important aspects of a person's actual lived experience. Such narratives are the most constrictive and often lead clients to seek out psychotherapy in the first place. EFT therapists must help these clients identify and elaborate their *unique outcome stories*, which challenge the underlying negative expectations and assumptions of clients' same old stories and problem-focused self-identity narratives. Specifically, limitations of the predominant problem-focused self-narrative are explored and challenged by the identification and elaboration of positive outcome stories that highlight clients' adaptive capacities to form deep and satisfying interpersonal relationships as well as to meet important goals and achievement outcomes. Sensing and "seeing" new possibilities for the resolution of problematic life concerns in turn engenders a hopeful expectancy for change and a heightened willingness to take action in the world.

In an intensive case analysis of 10 therapy dyads drawn from the York I Depression Study, more than 5 times as many unique outcome stories were coded for recovered clients than for nonrecovered clients (Bryntwick, Angus, Boritz, & Greenberg, 2011). Most notable, in the final phase of therapy, recovered clients articulated 8 times as many unique outcome stories as their nonrecovered counterparts.

It seems that therapeutic change may be concretized during the late phase of EFT through client expression, elaboration, and differentiation of positive and distinctive intra- and interpersonal experiences. Recovered clients demonstrated a much stronger tendency to engage in this process.

Stories that represent unique positive outcomes may also destabilize the negative expectations of a client's same old story and provoke a radical reauthoring of the client's self-narrative along more agentic and compassionate emotional plotlines. Hence, we think it is of critical importance that EFT therapists are responsive to the emergence of unique story outcome markers for the facilitation of heightened client meaning making and self-narrative identity reconstruction. In the process of identifying and refining narrative-emotion emergent meaning markers in the context of the York I Depression Study, two kinds of unique outcome story markers emerged: unexpected outcome stories and self-identity change stories.

Unexpected Outcome Stories

An *unexpected outcome story* is a personal story about a surprising event or unexpected outcome (e.g., feeling, action, hot thought) that documents a positive change in the client's daily life. Indicators of this include (a) positive differences in a client's behavior or psychological and emotional well-being, whether such differences are noticed by the client or by a significant other; (b) a client's articulation of a new sense or experience of the self in the world, including concomitant cognitions, emotions, and bodily sensations; (c) a client's comparisons between past and present behavior, emotional responses of surprise or delight, or thought patterns, as indicated by phrases such as "Whereas before"; (d) a client's expression of surprise, excitement, contentment, or inner peace; and (e) a client's paralinguistic cues, such as frequent smiling, laughing, or deep, satisfied breathing.

At markers of unexpected outcome, therapists notice and heighten clients' experience of positive difference and change. They encourage clients to elaborate and amplify what happened to create a full account of the newness and draw out and emphasize clients' contributions and agency in the change. This is all done in a curious, inquiring manner.

The following example of an unexpected story outcome marker was identified in Session 2 with one recovered EFT client from the York I Depression Study.

Client: The good thing last week was that, like, right now I don't feel responsible, like, for this person and, um, who moved out. There was always the split of, well, should I care, or should I, should I make an attempt to contact him and say, "Well, things just didn't work." I always feel responsible for other people and like mothering them and making sure they are OK and so on and so on, and just, like, I'm really tired of it, and I guess that was the first thing, like, just to say, "OK, your stuff is still here. It's not up to me to worry about it anymore."

Therapist: Well, you, I mean, it sounds like you were—the alarm bells went off and you knew what you wanted and needed and you did something about it so, that's certainly . . .

Client: And not feeling guilty about it.

Therapist: Yeah, that's the part you're happy about, that you did it but you're not feeling guilty about it.

Client: Oh yes, that's really, that's really great.

It is striking that already at Session 2 this EFT client is beginning to identify new, more satisfying emotional outcomes occurring in the context of interpersonal situations that would have caused feelings of anxiety and distress in the past. For this client in particular, the discovery that she could experience herself as a caring and worthwhile woman without always taking care of the needs of others was a revelation. The attuned and responsive therapist skillfully affirms the importance of this new development in the client's life by reflecting the actions she took—"Alarm bells went off and you knew what you wanted and needed and did something about it"—and linking them with the positive emotional outcomes—"That's the part you are happy about, that you did it and you are not feeling guilty about it."

Another unexpected story outcome marker was identified in a late phase EFT session. In Session 16, the client recollected a positive and unanticipated experience that she had during a job interview:

It was just really surprising and amazing, like, to see that—you know—and to notice that I just took a completely different approach to, uh, answering the question and representing, like, what's important to me. I was very pleased with myself.

In this example, the client indicates her surprise and amazement over her performance and seems to feel an invigorating sense of accomplishment. In addition, she acknowledges pride in her achievement, remarking, "I was very pleased with myself." This statement helps to cement the unexpected event as something meaningful and noteworthy. The therapist at this point affirms the change and asks her to elaborate on it and experience her joy.

Self-Identity Change Stories

The second, even more striking, subcategory of unique outcome story is termed the *self-identity change story*. Self-identity change stories are identified when clients describe a positive transformation in the overall narrative plotline of their life story and, perhaps most important, their view of self. Indicators are (a) the emergence of a new view of self and (b) client narrative reconstruction of personal identity. At a marker of self-identity change, the therapist facilitates the thematic integration of this new view and explores the significance of the new view of self for future life possibilities and choices. Clearly, elaboration of unique outcome stories leads to heightened awareness and integration of strengths and possibilities. ABMs organized according to self-defining themes provide us with a sense of who we were and who we are and give us a sense of purpose, unity, and identity. In this regard, an understanding of the self through time influences the way in which the past is constructed, and the way in which the past is constructed influences the way in which the self is conceptualized, in an ongoing dialectical fashion. Hence, the capacity to narrativize, understand, and integrate our most important life stories is key to adaptive identity development and the establishment of a differentiated, coherent view of self.

In a similar vein, Gonçalves, Mendes, Ribeiro, Angus, and Greenberg (2010) used the term *innovative moments* (i-moments) to categorize moments when clients are able to both identify and reflect on the impact of experiencing exceptions to the same old story during therapy sessions for their view of self. For these authors, reconceptualization moments represent a reauthoring position of the self wherein a client is now able to narrate their experiences of emotional transformation as an author of that change. The client is not only an actor of that process but also its author (Sarbin, 1986). Moreover, in the context of evaluating depressed clients undergoing EFT for depression, Mendes, Ribeiro, Angus, Greenberg, Sousa, and Goncalves (2010) reported that good outcome clients evidence a significantly higher proportion of reconceptualization i-moments in their therapy sessions than poor outcome clients, and they tend to elaborate those moments much more fully than their poor client counterparts.

In the following example of a self-identity change story marker, taken from the final session of a good outcome EFT, the client articulates her experience of emotional transformation and the experience of a new corrective experience of self that has emerged from her involvement in therapy. In an independent study this was also identified by Gonçalves, Mendes, Ribeiro, Angus, and Greenberg (2010) as meeting criteria for what was called the *moment of a reconceptualization*.

> *Client:* Yeah, yeah, get back into my feelings; yeah, and that's, I guess, because the awareness I know is there now, and before I never knew it existed [laughs], so I'm an individual. I realize I'm an individual and I have the right to vent my feelings and what I think is right or good for me, and that's been the improvement of the therapy, like, that I think, to me and myself.
>
> *Therapist:* Yeah, really finding your feet.
>
> *Client:* Mm-hmm, as an individual. Yeah, which before I, I thought I was glued to him [laughs]. Yeah, I didn't have an existence, and now I do, and that's a good feeling.

The client in this example clearly makes contrasts between her previous self and her present self, elaborating the change process beneath it. In so doing, she challenges a strong familial and cultural norm that a woman's first priority should be meeting the needs of others and that dissent should be silenced in the interest of family cohesion and loyalty. In the final phase of therapy, in reconceptualization i-moments, the client spent even more time elaborating the changes that she was able to make during the therapeutic process, assuming the authoring of change and the construction of a new narrative of the self.

The following excerpt comes from Session 8 with a recovered client. In this example, the client begins to feel entitled to look after her own needs and no longer feels the overwhelming desire to please others irrespective of the personal costs, thus challenging a strong cultural norm that had shaped her familial life for many years (i.e., her same old story).

> *Client:* I'm the perfect caregiver and caretaker, like, when it comes to other people. And I mean, I have always—well, I have known it for some time—but I don't know, but just by saying that and kind of, like, and thinking a little bit about it, like, it's all of sudden, like, no, like, I should be first before anybody else comes and, well, it's just almost like shifting

                gears, like getting used to that, so I feel kind of really excited about it.

Therapist: Yeah, yeah, it sounds really exciting to feel more centered in yourself and somehow to know that you do come first and to be able to act on that.

Although both client and therapist contribute to the coconstruction of a new view of self—"more centered in yourself and somehow to know that you do come first and be able to act on that"—the therapist also evocatively heightens the client's experience of excitement that conveys the importance of this new development for the client.

In response to the therapist's evocative and supportive empathic response, the client articulates the important emotional impact and consequences of her self-identity transformation.

Client: And it's just like discovering, like, a completely new world.

Therapist: It's like a new dimension that you were never really tuned into.

Client: It's just, like, such a relief, like, to get away from that, and I can feel like I just get so much more energy, a lot less tension, for sure.

Therapist: You're just sort of in yourself, like a deep breath is.

Client: Yeah, absolutely. It's just, like, where have you been?

In this instance, the client made reference to new bodily feelings associated with her unique outcome, remarking, "I just get so much more energy, a lot less tension, for sure." The therapist captured her affective experience quite adeptly through metaphor, stating, "You're just sort of in yourself, like a deep breath is." This client's same old story (i.e., pleasing others) was eventually jettisoned by her unique outcome stories in the middle and late phases of therapy.

HEALING STORIES

A *healing story* is a specific ABM narrative that conveys the feeling of having experienced positive emotions such as love, security, warmth, affection, and trust, toward and from a significant other (or significant others). These feelings transform the self into feeling whole, at peace, calm, and content. As these were often long forgotten memories, clients sometimes express surprise at having previously experienced these events. At these points, therapists need to focus on the newly accessed memory of feeling loved and heighten the felt experience of receiving care. In addition, the positive meaning of the experience is elaborated to restructure the narrative. The result of this is the restorying of narrative toward the possibility of having one's needs responded to.

The following example occurred in a mid-therapy session with a recovered client, who recalls her relationship with her grandfather with fond affection:

Client: Yeah, remembering how I would sit, like, really right next to him or, like, on his lap, and it's just feeling good, it's just like having this deep sense of security, like everything is all right now, there wasn't really anything to worry about or to get upset about; like, this is just great right now.

Therapist: So, it sounds like getting a real clear sense of you feeling kind of being loved and protected.

Client: Yeah, loved, protected, accepted. I guess, like, first I thought, like, there really never had been anything like that.

This example illustrates the positive emotions that the client felt both toward and from her grandfather. The client alludes to having forgotten these events for a long time and seems somewhat surprised that she had previously experienced such a positive and loving relationship, stating, "I guess, like, first I thought, like, there really never had been anything like that."

The next example of a healing story marker occurred in the seventh session of another good outcome EFT dyad.

Client: When I ask myself what is the matter, when I ask myself what it isn't, um, the issue that now comes to surface is the, is, is uh, I remember when I was with the other person. I mean it was so completely different.

Therapist: Mm-hmm, you used to feel loved.

Client: Oh, a whole different area of different feelings but, but never sadness [sniffs], never sadness.

Therapist: You felt alive.

Client: I felt more; first of all with him I felt like a Christmas tree—do you know how? I don't know how he makes me feel [laughs].

Therapist: All lit up?

Client: A Christmas tree might feel, but I, uh, but I always thought, like, I felt like a Christmas tree.

Therapist: Mm-hmm, just all lit up and . . .

Client: First of all, I was able to communicate perfectly. Secondly, I was able to be more, to be myself [sniffs] because I knew I was not going to be judged at all.

Therapist: So, very free. Yeah, it's like you're still longing for . . .

Client: For that type of relationship. Oh, yes.

Therapist: For that kind of connection again.

The emergence of a healing story during a therapy session can be an excellent opportunity to help the client fully articulate the fundamental importance of core attachment needs in their lives (i.e., to be loved and to matter). Healing stories can serve as a powerful exception to the negative expectations or rules of a client's same old story and open the door for the anticipation of future possibilities and satisfying relationships. For instance, one EFT client, Alex, who is discussed more fully in Chapter 7 of this volume, disclosed the following memories to her therapist in an empty-chair dialogue in which she is enacting and giving voice to the experience of her mother.

Client: You, you had a real nick in you there. You always had a real answer for things; you were quite bright, and I had a hard time keeping up with you. You were very mischievous. Fortunately, you never harmed yourself but your teasing, your light-heartedness, and your sense of humor . . .

Therapist: So, it sounds like you're saying I found you quite a delightful little girl.

Client: Those were good times, those were really good times.

Therapist: Hmm, those are beautiful memories.

Client: I would take you to the lake and going to my, to Grandma's house, helping Grandma with those donuts, and Grandma would be there baking, and you adored the pets, the animals that you had. That cat—God, I couldn't stand that cat, but you insisted on keeping that ratty old cat, and the mice under your bed. That was [laughs], I don't know.

Therapist: Sounds like it warms your heart to think of those things.

Client: There were a lot of good times, too, and it is difficult not to be negative and think of it in a negative way. It's . . .

Therapist: But it's important.

Client: It's very important.

Therapist: Can you come over here? [Client changes chairs.] So how are you feeling? Warm and . . .

Client: Yeah, I feel warm and I feel secure.

Therapist: Can you say that to her?

Client: It does make me feel more secure, loved. I liked feeling like that; it felt nice. Since you died, I have not been able to really feel that. I think I have to challenge everybody and everything.

It is significant that it was only after Alex had been able to forgive her mother's decision to commit suicide when Alex was a 12-year-old child that these tender memories of a loving engagement between mother and daughter are recalled and disclosed in her therapy sessions. As demonstrated in the foregoing example, the therapist's empathic responses play an important role in the client's sustained elaboration of her loving memories. In addition, the therapist's inquiry "So how are you feeling?" in response to disclosing the memories helps the client both to feel the warmth and to symbolize this soothing emotion in awareness and reflect on the importance of the feelings of warm and trust that are evoked by her recollections. This shift to a more positive emotion and positive ABMs, rather than her previous feeling of being cold and clammy, led to the construction of a new narrative of a loving rather than an uncaring mother. In addition, the therapist's request to have the client tell her mother about these feelings enhances the sense of a loving bond and attachment connection between daughter and mother, a feeling that had not been experienced since her mother's sudden death many years ago. To facilitate the development of a more integrative and compassionate view of herself in relation to her mother, the therapist might ask Alex, "And what does this mean to you, that you were loved by your mom as a little girl?" The capacity to be able to return to these recollections in the future, and to the imagined conversation with her mother, sets the stage for self-narrative reconstruction wherein Alex may begin to reintegrate a sense of having been loved by a mother who made a tragic mistake and asks for forgiveness.

CONCLUSION

Untold stories, unique outcome stories, and healing stories highlight the presence of emergent meaning opportunities for therapists working with clients in EFT. Each of these markers represents the emergence of a different kind of "new development" in the client's self-story that requires different therapist strategies for further integration and self-narrative reconstruction. The emergence and articulation of untold stories—specific, emotion-charged ABM narratives with negative emotional plotlines—often addresses important gaps in the client's explicit self-narrative. Untold stories are often lived stories that have been too painful, shameful, or frightening for clients to disclose to another person. Clients often feel as if they are being held hostage by these powerful emotional memories and engage in active emotional avoidance in an attempt to limit awareness of these painful events and their emotional consequences. Once an untold story marker has been identified, a key therapist goal is to help clients allow awareness of the painful lived story to enable further narrative contextualization, emotional transformation, and new meaning construction.

Unique outcome stories are specific ABM narratives of recent events that represent positive, unanticipated emotional and relational outcomes that challenge the negative plotlines and experiential stuckness of the client's same old story. Unique outcome stories indicate when clients are actually trying new ways of being in the world and beginning to experience positive relational and emotional outcomes as a result. Unique outcome stories are powerful destabilizers of the client's same old story because they instantiate irrefutable evidence that clients can achieve previously unexpected positive emotional and relational outcomes in their lives when they are able to take a risk and try to do so. Of key importance for long-term, sustained change is helping clients to provide fuller accounts of their own contributions to the genesis of the positive story outcomes, which highlights the importance of these events for a satisfying and sustaining life. Moreover, the simple occurrence of the unique outcome story is a serious challenge to the overgeneralized negative expectations and plotlines of the client's same old story that brought them to therapy in the first place. Often, unique outcome stories instantiate cherished values, attributes, and/or meanings for the client that are also important to identify as a new view of self and to integrate as part of the client's self-narrative.

Healing story markers are characterized by the disclosure of positive, attachment-related memories that sustain a client's experience of having been loved, cherished, and cared for by significant others in the past. As with untold stories, clients often have difficulty retrieving or returning to positive relational memories of the past (i.e., healing stories) as they challenge the core negative emotional plotline of neglect, victimization, or incompetence that has sustained the client's same old story for many years. Like unique outcome stories, healing stories provide both client and therapist with rich opportunities to challenge and destabilize the seemingly inevitable negative expectations and emotions of the same old story and, in so doing, articulate a new, more compassionate view of self that results in a more differentiated, yet coherent, self-narrative.

6

WORKING WITH NARRATIVE AND EMOTION IN DEPRESSION: THE CASE OF MARGARET

This chapter presents a case example of one recovered client from the York I Depression Study. This example demonstrates the effectiveness of narrative-informed emotion-focused therapy (EFT) therapists' work with client problem-focused and emergent meaning markers in treating depression. The chapter begins with an overview of depression from a narrative-emotion perspective followed by an overview of treating empty stories, same old stories, and broken stories, the predominant problem markers emerging in this case study. We then discuss the four phases of treatment that occurred for this case study.

OVERVIEW OF DEPRESSION FROM A NARRATIVE-EMOTION PERSPECTIVE

Emerging research evidence from both the cognitive-experimental (Williams et al., 2007) and psychotherapy research literature (Boritz, Angus, Monette, & Hollis-Walker, 2008) has indicated that a key cognitive marker of clinical depression is a preference for overgeneral autobiographical memory (ABM) representations, with difficulty accessing and disclosing specific or episodic ABM narratives of personal life events. This is important because the inability to access and integrate specific episodic ABMs has been associated with reduced self-coherence, increased rumination and worry, impairment in social problem solving, and a reduced capacity to imagine future events (Conway & Pleydell-Pearce, 2000). It is interesting that cognitive researchers such as Teasdale (1999) have suggested that overgeneral memory representations may function as an effective emotion avoidance strategy (Boritz, Angus, Monette, & Hollis-Walker, 2011) that results in impaired specific ABM recall and negatively impacts effective problem solving and the articulation of new personal meanings. Taken together, these findings suggest that therapists' ability to help clients move to more specific ABM disclosures in therapy sessions may be a key emotion processing step—and change event—in effective treatments of depression.

Boritz et al. (2008) examined the contributions of ABM specificity in two early, two middle, and two late sessions drawn from 17 emotion-focused and 17 client-centered treatments of depression. Using the Narrative Processes Coding System (Angus, Levitt, & Hardtke, 1999), raters first identified narratives that met criteria as a personal ABM and then rated those narratives for degree of specificity: single event, generic, or eventless. Research findings established that ABM specificity significantly increased for the sample as a whole from early to late phase sessions. Further analyses (Boritz et al., 2011) indicated that recovered clients who achieved clinically significant change at therapy termination consistently achieved significantly higher levels of expressed emotions in their specific ABM narratives than clients who remained symptomatic or unchanged at therapy termination.

OVERVIEW OF TREATMENT: WORKING WITH SAME OLD STORIES, EMPTY STORIES, AND BROKEN STORIES

As noted in Chapter 4, the same old story is often represented by an overgeneral ABM narrative that summarizes a series of past lived events in terms of a core maladaptive emotional scheme. Although the characters and setting may change, the maladaptive emotional plotlines of the same old story remain the same over time. The same old story sustains negative emotional plotlines in the depressed client's life and often revolves around key personal relationships (e.g., parents, siblings, a spouse, the self) and represents deeply held identity beliefs embedded in emotion schemes (e.g., "Even as a kid I would feel like—you know—I'm not a particularly likeable person"). In addition, the same old story rarely contains new positive outcomes (e.g., "My mother was very supportive this time") or memories and is quite undifferentiated and stale, as though it has been well rehearsed by the client and leaves little room for the possibility of adaptive change. In light of depressed clients' propensity to access overgeneral memory recall, it should not be surprising to discover that they are highly adept at expressing same old stories during their therapy sessions. It seems as though depressed clients who articulated same old stories felt trapped by their own life experience(s) and could not see alternative explanations of events or choices for the future.

In a recent set of intensive case analyses of three clients who recovered from depression versus three clients who remained unchanged after brief EFT treatment, Bryntwick, Angus, Boritz, and Greenberg (2011) found that same old stories were the most common narrative and emotion subtype occurring in psychotherapy sessions drawn from the York I Depression Study. Same old stories seemed to occur most frequently during the middle and later phases of EFT for clients who had not recovered from depression by therapy termination. Specifically, EFT clients who recovered from depression by therapy termination accounted for 37% of the total number of same old stories, whereas 63% of the total was found in the transcripts of nonrecovered EFT clients. Moreover, nonrecovered clients articulated more than twice as many same old stories in the early phase of therapy compared with their recovered counterparts (22 vs. nine, respectively) and expressed more than 3 times as many in the late phase (19 vs. six, respectively).

In particular, Bryntwick et al. (2011) found that clients who recovered from clinical depression evidenced a greater awareness of being "stuck" in an intra- or interpersonal maladaptive pattern that they themselves were perpetuating in some important way. As such, recovered EFT clients seemed to take more ownership of their same old stories and stand in opposition or protest against them. For example, the following depressed client who recovered at therapy termination stated that although she was aware that she suppressed her own feelings of optimism and hope in an effort to protect herself from pain, she did not want her children to suffer a similar debilitating fate. The following is an excerpt from Session 3 of her therapy.

> *Client:* I anticipate too many problems. I think I'm squishing the ability to be optimistic out of my kids, sending signals: "Well, don't get too excited." I'll be a wet blanket on things like "You shouldn't be too happy." Why am I giving that to them?
>
> *Therapist:* Seems like you're really concerned about that kind of belief that, that you sort of grew up with, is gonna sort of be transferred to your children, and you seem to really not want that to happen, and it hurts you to see that happen.
>
> *Client:* Mm-hmm, no, I don't want them to do that. Yeah, to see any of the—you know—as I say, with my oldest saying, "I hate my life," I can just, I just see myself sitting there, you know?

Therapist: So you see yourself in her?

Client: Yeah, exactly. Too much, too much.

In this session excerpt, the client is identifying an emotionally painful interpersonal pattern, or emotion scheme, that is both maladaptive and recurring, stating, "I anticipate too many problems. I think I'm squishing the ability to be optimistic out of my kids." She acknowledges her own complicity in its perpetuation, remarking, "[I'm] sending signals: 'Well, don't get too excited.' . . . Why am I giving that to them?" In addition, there is also a hint of protest in the client's story, as though she is beginning to mobilize her energy to fight against the same old story of starving her feelings of hope and excitement. When her EFT therapist reflects that the client does not want to pass down her pessimistic attitude toward life to her children, she remarks, "No, I don't want them to do that," as though she is gearing up for a change in action and plotline.

Bryntwick et al. (2011) also noted in intensive case analyses that clients who recovered from depression appear to feel less victimized by their own circumstances and, as a result, are often less critical of others in general. As such, recovered clients were more likely to discuss important unmet needs and their emotional implications with their EFT therapists, as opposed to dwelling on the failings of a significant other. For example, one EFT client who recovered from depression expressed her feelings of not being loved by her mother as her own unmet need.

Therapist: Uh-huh, uh-huh, you feel sadness.

Client: Yes, and um . . .

Therapist: Remembering not feeling loved.

Client: No, or um, it was never expressed, it was never, um, said to me.

Therapist: Uh-huh, tell her, tell your mom that, that you wanted to hear it.

Client: Um, I wanted to hear you say that um you loved me.

Therapist: Mm-hmm. Tell her what it was like for you.

Client: Um, it was lonely and, um [sniffs], um, confusing. Yeah, it just, um, knowing that, um, I, I did as you said, and, um, I always tried to please you, but, um, you never, um, expressed your love.

Therapist: Mm-hmm, mm-hmm. This feeling seems to be, um, you feel a lot of sadness.

Client: Yeah.

Therapist: And not feeling her love coming to you.

Rather than blaming her mother for being inadequate, the client expresses to her mother, within the context of an EFT empty-chair intervention, how she had never felt the love she so desperately needed. Bryntwick et al. (2011) highlighted how the EFT therapist helped the client to more fully enter and differentiate the emotional landscape of her same old story with statements such as "Tell your mom what it is that you wanted to hear," "Tell her what it was like for you," "You feel a lot of sadness and her love not coming to you" in the context of the empty-chair intervention. Bryntwick et al. suggested that this prompting helps the client to reflexively explore the emotional consequences of her unmet relational needs. When working with the same old stories of clients who recover from depression, effective EFT therapists thus appear to focus more keenly on the client's emotional experience of the story, as opposed to its maladaptive content. In the next example from Session 3, the therapist asks the client to describe her emotional experience of not feeling supported by her parents.

Client: I mean, that has been, uh, that has been around, like, all the way through my childhood that, um, my parents really never supported me, like, with things which were important to me.

Therapist: So, somehow then, I wonder how that felt, them giving you these messages and you not feeling they were right for you. It must have felt . . .

Client: Ah, well, well, pretty terrible actually.

As evidenced in this example, the EFT therapist does not focus on the client's negative portrayal of her parents but instead tries to understand the idiosyncratic emotional responses and personal meanings that this experience evokes for the client, with questions such as, "So, somehow then, I wonder how that felt, them giving you these messages." Focusing on or validating the content, as opposed to differentiating the emotional experience of the same old story, may only serve to strengthen its power over the client.

Finally, Bryntwick et al. (2011) suggested that EFT therapists of recovered clients seem to be, on average, more tentative in their phrasing of a client's same old story (e.g., using phrases such as "it feels," as opposed to "it is") and are therefore far less likely to run the risk of authoring their client's story for them, as demonstrated in the following example.

Client: I'm starting to get scared, panicky, again. Yeah, I'm starting to panic. Like, what if—you know—something happens and I don't have anybody around? Oh, my God!

Therapist: Yeah, what? How did that sit with you?

Client: I don't know, but this, is this always going to happen? I don't know [sighs].

Therapist: It feels like it, there's no end to this, or you can't imagine not worrying like this.

Client: Yeah, yeah, I can't imagine being—you know—just relaxed, just not thinking of anything.

As Bryntwick et al. (2011) noted, the EFT therapist's tentative, empathic responses "It feels like there is no end to this" and "You can't imagine not worrying like this" help the client to reflect on her own overlearned maladaptive emotional responses as one way—currently, her way—of experiencing the situation and, by default, suggesting that alternative responses are by definition possible. In essence, although the experience feels as though it will never end and the client cannot imagine overcoming her anxiety, the possibility exists that this could happen.

When compared with EFT clients who recovered from depression, Bryntwick et al. (2011) found that depressed clients who were unchanged at therapy termination tended to place more blame on significant others for having wronged them in their same old stories and, during their therapy sessions, focused their attention much more fully on the transgressions of others. For example, the following depressed client was in an unhappy marriage, and in this excerpt, taken from the late phase of her therapy, she blames her husband for her inability to be herself in the relationship and the suffering she endured as a result.

Therapist: Yeah, so that you can really notice when you're not with him you feel . . .

Client: When I am not with him, I can be myself.

Therapist: Ah, so, being with him . . .

Client: Doesn't allow me . . .

Therapist: You don't feel you can be yourself.

Client: No, because he, he keeps being, um, all the things that just made me so miserable all these years, and it's still bothering me.

Therapist: Mm-hmm, that somehow these things just aren't going away and it still somehow really bothers you.

Client: Yeah, because they will never go away.

In this example, the client is placing full responsibility for her unhappiness on her husband, stating, "He keeps being, um, all the things that just made me so miserable all these years, and it's still bothering me." Moreover, this client remained externally focused throughout the course of therapy and did not often evaluate her own dysfunctional behavior in the marriage or her unique contributions to the discordant home environment and her current feelings of depression. For many of the nonrecovered depressed clients in the study, acknowledging their own role in the maintenance of their same old stories appeared somewhat difficult.

On the few occasions that unchanged depressed clients did identify experiencing a reprieve from their maladaptive intra- or interpersonal patterns during a therapy session, that admission was swiftly dismissed and swallowed up by the negative, predominating theme of the same old story. Bryntwick et al. (2011) identified the following example as exemplifying this pattern.

Therapist: It's important for you in your life at times to try and make the right impression or win the approval of particular people.

Client: Win approval; I would like to be liked more than I am. [Pauses] I guess as a result, I, most of my life I try to behave so that I please others, and in the last couple of years I've tried to drop that. I'm not treating myself bad. Things that I talked about last week—trying to be appropriate, trying to fit in and sacrificing my own values instead—I don't want to do that anymore, but then I have to face the pain all over again that what I do put out is not liked, generally, I mean; most, no, in the majority of cases.

The client's brief discussion about subverting her same old story—"Most of my life I try to behave so that I please others, and in the last couple of years I've tried to drop that. I'm not treating myself bad"—was followed almost immediately by an expression of defeat as she rearticulated her bleak interpersonal prospects, stating, "I don't want to do that anymore, but then I have to face the pain all over again that what I do put out is not liked."

Therapists should try to carefully avoid becoming trapped in the negative content of same old stories. For example, one therapist focused a great deal of attention on the content and circumstances of her client's same old story, validating the client's perception of her living conditions as unbearable, rather than exploring the emotional experience of those conditions and the unmet relational needs that they conveyed.

Therapist: I think the feeling that is so strong as I'm listening to you is that I wish I could change this for you, I wish I could come in there and just whip the kids into shape—get you the kind of living conditions you wanted, I mean. I hear about what you have to live with, and I would find it intolerable. I don't know how you've managed to survive.

Client: I'm always in the catch-22 because I've never believed myself to be weak, to be incapable of handling things, but I'm in a situation where I'm not sure it's my fault that the situation is there, and I'm not sure I can deal with it much longer. Eventually somebody's going to break, either the kids or me.

Although it is likely that the therapist's remark was an attempt to align herself with the client, the client appeared to be feeling powerless to manage or change her circumstances. In addition, her own role in the situation remained unexplored because the therapist externalized the source of the problem. This robbed the client of an all-important sense of personal agency and control in transforming her own same old story.

In light of these important clinical research findings, we felt that the next important step was to identify specific emotion and narrative markers that would facilitate effective treatment interventions when working with depressed clients in narrative-informed EFT. Specifically, facilitating client shifts from overgeneral memory recall—often expressed as same old stories—to productive experiential engagement during therapy sessions was a key goal in this effort. More specifically, it is essential that narrative-informed EFT therapists help depressed clients more fully experientially enter and vivify empty stories for the articulation of maladaptive emotion schemes and primary emotional responses and adaptive action tendencies.

One of the key indicators of an *empty story* is the abundance of superfluous details about the circumstances of an event, often sounding like a laundry list of "what happened," with little substantive reflexivity or emotional language. In the context of her intensive case analyses of EFT treatments of depression, Bryntwick et al. (2011) found that the frequency of empty stories varied considerably across recovered and nonrecovered outcome groups. Overall, recovered clients contributed 20% of empty stories, whereas nonrecovered clients were responsible for 80% of all empty stories identified in the transcript sample. However, when examined by phase of therapy, recovered clients evidenced a decline in number of empty stories articulated as therapy progressed (50% occurred in the early phase compared with 17% in the late phase), whereas nonrecovered clients articulated roughly the same number of empty stories in both the early and late phases of therapy (nine vs. 10, respectively). Bryntwick et al. noted that nonrecovered clients tended to somaticize the problem instead of addressing the emotional implications of an empty story (e.g., when discussing a deep depression, a client would reveal only physical symptoms, such as decreased appetite and disturbed sleep, and not the emotional toll of the experience). As such, it appears that the recounting of empty stories may function to keep the client at a safe distance from emotional pain and injury and can thus be conceptualized as a defense mechanism similar to repression.

As elaborated in Chapter 4, it is suggested that therapists help clients become emotionally engaged with the lived experience of their empty stories rather than provide a disengaged chronicle of the circumstances of what happened. Evocative empathy and focusing interventions are both used to engage a fuller bodily felt awareness of the emotional impact of the story—especially with respect to adaptive emotions—and help clients to articulate the personal significance of the event. When the subjective experiencing of an event can be coherently integrated with the circumstances of what happened, clients are able to achieve a deepened understanding of the impact of the event. Moreover, the activation and articulation of adaptive emotions helps clients to take actions in the world to satisfy unmet interpersonal needs and achieve new story outcomes.

In addition, helping depressed clients to challenge and then reauthor their same old stories as broken stories was identified as a key transitional step toward the emergence of unexpected outcome stories and recovery from depression. Emotionally distressing personal memories and overpowering and contradictory emotions often interfere with a narrator's attempts to organize the experience as a coherent story that can be subsequently shared with others and reflected on for further self-understanding.

In a recent set of intensive case analyses of three clients who recovered from depression versus three clients who remained unchanged after brief EFT treatment, Bryntwick et al. (2011) found that broken stories were the third most common narrative and emotion subtype found in the sample (31 in total). Specifically, recovered clients articulated more than twice as many broken stories as those clients in the nonrecovered group (22 vs. nine, respectively). This finding suggests that broken stories, particularly those involving conflicting emotional responses, may be important to the process of recovery from depression. Rather than remaining stuck in the same old story scheme, clients who are on the verge of therapeutic change may have a more acute awareness of conflicting emotional plotlines and intentions, which enhances a commitment to work toward swift resolution of their chaotic emotional experience.

In psychotherapy, a depressed client's inability to successfully organize and integrate the conflicting emotions and actions experienced in the context of troubling events represents the definitive broken story in which the client's thoughts and feelings about disturbing life events have remained fragmented, disconnected, and "not understood." Distressing memories of loss, shame, and humiliation may resist assimilation to a client's preexisting self-narrative and require the implementation of marker-guided interventions to facilitate emotional integration, story coherence, and behavior change. As Bryntwick et al. (2011) noted, many of the recovered clients in the EFT sample seemed to possess a keen awareness of a struggle between two competing emotional reactions, or parts of the self, in the context of expressing their broken story during therapy sessions, and this is certainly evidenced in the case of Margaret, which is the focus of this chapter. Furthermore, as evidenced in the following case analysis, it is often the case that when the EFT therapist expresses one side of the conflict and the client expresses another, a more compassionate and empowering dialogue emerges between the competing emotional plotlines, which results in the expression of primary adaptive emotions and action tendencies that in turn facilitate enacting new story outcomes.

The following case example of Margaret (Angus & Hardtke, 2007), a client who recovered from depression in the context of the York I Depression Study, demonstrates how narrative-emotion markers—in particular, same old story, empty stories, and broken stories—can provide a helpful therapeutic framework for the implementation of effective treatment interventions for the amelioration of clinical depression. The four key phases of narrative-informed EFT—(a) facilitating bonding, narrative unfolding, and awareness; (b) facilitating evocation, exploration, and articulation of narrative themes; (c) facilitating transformation of emotion and new story outcomes; and (d) facilitating consolidation and narrative reconstruction—are also identified and provide a guiding framework for the effective application of narrative-emotion markers.

CLINICAL CASE ANALYSIS

Margaret was a 58-year-old Caucasian who was a married, full-time homemaker living with her husband, Carl, and daughter, Dalia, at the time of her participation in the York I Depression Study. Although she took pride in her role as an active caregiver for her immediate family and aging parents, recent events had led to many changes in her daily life. Her father had recently died and her elderly mother required nursing home care for a degenerative neurological disorder. In addition, her daughter was soon to be married and leaving the family home. And perhaps most significant, Margaret reported experiencing a growing sense of frustration and disconnection in her marriage, in which she felt unsupported in her efforts to "keep the family together." Her husband's increasing focus on new work responsibilities also added to her sense of feeling neglected and taken for granted by him.

Prior to starting treatment, Margaret met criteria for major depressive disorder (Structured Clinical Interview for *DSM III–R*; Spitzer, Williams, Gibbons, & First, 1989) and completed a battery of standardized pre- and postassessment measures that included the Beck Depression Inventory (BDI; Beck, 1976) and the Symptom Checklist-90-Revised (SCL-90-R; Derogatis, Rickels, & Roch, 1976). Margaret's BDI scores dropped from 21 at the start of the study to 12 at the conclusion of her therapy sessions. Moreover, clinically significant improvement was evidenced by the Global Symptom index of the SCL-90-R, with a drop from 1.30 to 0.47. Importantly, Margaret no longer met criteria for major depressive disorder (Spitzer et al., 1989) at therapy termination. Treatment consisted of 17 one-hour audio- and videotaped therapy sessions. Her therapist was rated as demonstrating high levels of empathy, understanding, and attunement in selected therapy sessions.

Phase 1: Bonding, Narrative Unfolding, and Awareness

In her initial therapy session, Margaret first links the onset of her depression to a wide range of events that had occurred over a 1-year period of time:

> But, um, no, basically, um, my depression, I, like, I think is being, sort of, over the last 5 years, um, it just seemed that there was one year in my life that everything happened. Well, first of all, my son moved out to the city. Then I have a daughter too, but—you know—she was going to university at that point, so she wasn't really at home either. And then, um, I started having problems with my parents in that, um, my mother had arthritis and, um, I was, like, I come from a fairly big family, but I was the only one who didn't go to business, and I ended up looking after my parents.

In this chronicle of events, experiences are recounted in a disconnected, truncated manner that lacks a clear beginning, middle, and end and is stripped of emotional meaning or significance. These are the key characteristics of an empty story problem marker. Another feature of an empty story is that without emotional differentiation, the significance of the story remains unclear to the client, and this certainly is the case for Margaret. Both the lack of narrative elaboration detailing how or why these specific events are linked together and limited emotional expression make it difficult for Margaret and her therapist to understand how these disparate experiences are interconnected and what specific meaning they have for her in the context of her struggle with depression.

As noted earlier, carefully listening to clients' same old stories during early therapy sessions can help therapists to identify core maladaptive interpersonal themes and emotion schemes when formulating a case conceptualization and articulating key therapy goals. A key client indicator of a same old story marker is the feeling of being stuck in a repetitive cycle of resentment, bitterness, and complaint that is highly resistant to change. Such is the case during Session 1 when Margaret evocatively describes the same old story of her marriage, a vicious, emotional cycle of fear, hurt, and anger that she finds herself "caught" or "stuck in":

> I find it particularly with Carl—that's my husband—I know I can sort of let myself relax to a certain extent, and things go along and then I think, "Uh-uh, no one's going to do that to me again," and I think deep down I'm thinking "You're not going to hurt me." My way of expressing fear is

> that I get angry and I yell and I know I am not being a nice person; it bothers me somehow—you know—I think, "Why can't I be a nice person?"

Margaret's same old story evocatively captures a core maladaptive emotion scheme of her fear of rejection that she finds herself stuck in—and concerned about—yet helpless to change.

Phase 2: Evocation, Articulation of Narrative Themes, and Disclosure of Untold Stories

In response to Margaret's sparse narrative account, and in pursuit of deeper meaning regarding her same old story, the therapist first empathically validates how difficult that time must have been for her: "And it sounds like it was partly that there were just so many things happening to you, all at once." The therapist then invites her to disclose the specific event or experience that is most painful to disclose: "I wonder if there is any one thing that stands out as having been particularly hard to cope with in the year that everything happened?" In response to the therapist's invitation for an emotionally salient narrative disclosure, Margaret reveals for the first time that her husband Carl had also become increasingly engaged in new work responsibilities during that time, and she had come to feel quite neglected by him as a result:

> I look back on it. At the time I was very resentful because—you know—I felt all the responsibility was falling on me, and the result was that it came to a point that when our children left home, he started in on this job and he didn't have time to support me and I felt very neglected. I mean, he's wrapped up in his job and it's just . . . I know I don't understand it enough, like I just sort of feel like, "Hey, I've been giving, giving, giving to the kids and the husband for 30 odd years; when is it going to be my turn?"

With this disclosure, Margaret gives strong expression to feeling stuck in a maladaptive interpersonal pattern in which she feels that her emotional needs have been neglected by others, and she feels deeply resentful about that turn of events. Margaret's same old story, "Hey, I've been giving, giving, giving to the kids and the husband for 30 odd years; when is it going to be my turn?" powerfully conveys the long-standing feelings of resentment that she feels toward her husband. Although Margaret seems to connect her husband's increasing job responsibilities with feelings of emotional neglect, she states, "I don't understand it enough," and in so doing provides her therapist with an indicator that she is beginning to experience a sense of puzzlement wherein all of the pieces of her same old story no longer fit seamlessly together. In addition, Margaret seems to be starting to challenge the intractable stuckness of her emotionally unsatisfying same old story when she poignantly asks, "When is it going to be my turn?"—a strong indicator that she may be ready to begin working on restructuring her same old story.

As noted in Chapter 4, emotional incoherence broken story markers were identified significantly more often in fully recovered EFT clients who no longer met criteria for depression at therapy termination compared with EFT clients who remained clinically depressed at therapy termination. As in the case of Margaret, a client's growing sense of incoherence about their own same old stories, wherein the old pieces of the puzzle no longer seem to fit or make sense, may be an important indicator of client readiness for narrative change and for a more differentiated exploration of emotions, actions, intentions, and needs that used to be so easily encapsulated in the same old story. Helping clients to become curious about their own same old stories, finding specific ABM narratives in which the same old story "happens," and helping clients to emotionally enter those stories are all important ways in which effective EFT therapists can help clients challenge their own same old stories for the development of new, more rewarding, and agentic story outcomes. Markers of narrative coherence include (a) a clear sense of the beginning, middle, and end of the story; (b) descriptions of the internal subjective experiences of protagonists and antagonists; (c) an explicit understanding of causes or factors that contributed to conflicting emotions, actions, and intentions of self and others; and finally (d) an inner felt sense of resolution wherein the same old story is seen and experienced in a new, often more positive, light that promotes a heightened sense of personal agency, hope, and a willingness to try new actions and behaviors in the world.

Attuned to Margaret's feelings of puzzlement and dissatisfaction about her same old story, her therapist in the following empathic response tentatively proposes a plausible connection between "that time when everything happened" and her feelings of resentment and bitterness toward her husband: "Well, I'm not sure. Your sense is that you have been giving, especially in that year that everything happened all at once [*Client:* Mm-hmm.], and kind of now waiting to get something back and not just getting it."

With this empathic response, the therapist sets the stage for a new narrative contextualization of Margaret's bitter feelings of resentment toward her husband as an outcome of the lack of emotional support she received subsequent to the exceptional caring that she provided to others during "that year that everything happened." In essence, the therapist reflects a plausible connection between Margaret's inner hopes, needs, and feelings with specific events that occurred in her life. In so doing, the therapist scaffolds a possible retelling of Margaret's same old story of depression that now provides a causal connection between emotions felt and actions taken that now has a relational context (i.e., husband) and a temporal location (i.e., the year that everything happened) for the development of a heightened sense of narrative coherence and emotion-narrative integration.

It is striking to note that Margaret's early expression of emotional incoherence—"I just don't understand"—uttered in response to her own same old story of her marriage is an early indicator of the core relational issue that predominates throughout the middle phase of therapy. Specifically, both Margaret and her therapist engage in an extended exploration of her marital relationship and the confusing array of conflicting emotions (i.e., resentment, hurt, puzzlement) and possible action tendencies (e.g., pull away, attack, placate) they evoke in her. A key indicator that Margaret's same old story is beginning to transition and shift into a broken story is her feeling of confusion and puzzlement (i.e., "I just don't understand") and her acknowledgment, "I'm seesawing all the time like I can't seem to, I can't get a grip on how I feel."

In the following excerpt, Margaret articulates the heart of her broken story when she discloses how difficult it is to accept that her marriage may be "failing," while at the same time acknowledging the acute frustration she feels in relation to experiencing unmet interpersonal and emotional needs in her life.

Client: I think, actually, that it's actually gotten to the point that I question . . . I think maybe I want to go back to the way we were, but on the other hand, maybe it's because I don't want to admit that my marriage failed, and—you know, like, maybe—and then I think, well, maybe I don't love him anymore, but I don't think that's right, you know.

Therapist: So it doesn't feel right that you don't love him [*Client:* No], but it feels somehow that the—is this right?—that the pain is the sense of it's failed, this marriage; it can't go back?

Client: Yeah, I think this is it. So, the result is like I'm seesawing all the time like I can't seem to, I can't get a grip on how I feel, like, I can't—you know—I can't resolve it in my mind that OK, stop nagging; why does he irritate you so much? Like—you know—is it because of—you know—that sense of failure? Like, I mean, I don't think that anyone wants to admit that they've failed in anything—you know.

Therapist: So, somehow having failed in, like, you don't want to admit it's failed, so you get on him for things that he's doing wrong; is that it? But, really, it's almost a sense that you've failed somehow?

Client: No, I think it's a sense that we've failed—you know—like we've failed as a couple. You know, maybe I think, maybe this is more—you know—like this is not working and, um . . .

Therapist: And that seems like a very painful thing to have to realize.

Client: Yeah, to have to sort of face up to the fact that, gee, well, it didn't work. And I look at other people and I think—well, you know, um—and I envy them, but then I sometimes wonder if we're unique.

Therapist: There seems to be a lot of confusion; certainly, what comes across is whether or not you failed by any external standards, and also what comes across to me is your sense that it's not giving you what you want right now.

Client: You know, I, I hadn't really thought of it, like, in those words, you know, but maybe this is how I feel. Like right now I just—yes, you're right, there is, sometimes there is, a just a total, total frustration.

Therapist: Frustration, like it's just not right for me?

Client: Yeah, nothing seems to be going—you know—the way I want it to and, um, and then I think, well, on the other hand, maybe. I mean, this is just life—you know—and you can't always get what you want. And, um, and things just don't go your way and, um . . .

Therapist: So, maybe I have to just, maybe I should just resign myself to this? And then yet you go back to that sense of, it sounds like you keep going back to this "no, maybe things can change."

In the foregoing excerpt, the therapist helps Margaret to become more fully aware of the experiential consequences of her broken story and to acknowledge and accept that her deep frustration with her husband may be the outcome of important unmet interpersonal needs. In the following session, Margaret reports a recent incident that led to a new, positive experience of self in relation to her husband, and as such, meets the criteria as an emergent meaning marker. In the following unexpected outcome story, Margaret describes her awareness of a new, positive experience of self—"I have had a positive reaction in myself and how I am handling the situation"—that emerged when she was able to assert herself with her husband and directly protest his treatment of their son:

> I don't think this is all my problem right now, and it's the first time I've had a positive reaction in myself and how I'm handling this situation. I think, actually, I think I, I floored Carl when I said to him, "And you will." I—you know—I just, I said it in this tone: "You! Will! Not! Break up my family!" I said, "Because if you send my son away and I don't see my son," I said, "Then I'll leave too." I said, "Because you're not going to do that to me." I said, "It's too important to me." I said, "We will discuss it, like we did at Christmastime," and I said, "Maybe we can find a solution—you know—that we can handle it in the same way." I said, "But if we can't,

then we'll each handle it in our own way." A few months ago, I would not have been able to do that.

In the early phase therapy sessions, Margaret's initial empty story of the "one year in her life that everything happened" and same old story of emotional neglect from others evolved into the broken story of her marriage, wherein she acknowledges "seesawing" between deep frustrations of experiencing unmet needs with her husband while fearing at the same time being in a "failed" marriage. During mid-phase sessions, the narrative contextualization of Margaret's bitter feelings of resentment toward her husband—as an outcome of lack of emotional support from him—provides a new, more empowering understanding of her feelings of deep frustration and helps scaffold and support new efforts to assert her needs with her husband in real life. Thus, during this second stage, her resentment was evoked and she was helped to approach, accept, symbolize, and tolerate this and other emotions and use them for narrative-informed action.

Phase 3: Emotional Transformation and New Story Outcomes

At the start of Session 11, it is clear that both client and therapist are in agreement that the most important concern for Margaret to resolve in therapy is her feeling of bitterness and resentment toward her husband, Carl. It is at this point that an untold story marker emerges—one that eventually reveals a broken story of the deep hurt of being physically abused by her elderly mother—shattering her sense of sense of safety and security in a relationship of caring at the core of her experience:

> You know how we were talking last week: Like, the most important, the biggest thing in my life seems to be my problem with Carl. And that seems to be what I could resolve. Actually, if we could resolve—um, if we could be together, I think I could handle all the other tensions better.

In the session, as she begins to reflect on her marriage and recalls past memories, Margaret seeks reassurance from her therapist about the task at hand—that returning to the past will indeed be helpful to meet her current therapeutic goals.

Client: I don't know whether it is good to go back like this or not; is it?

Therapist: I think it is, because it sounds like you're still holding feelings from back then.

Client: If I could just let go of some of these feelings, I think I would be an awful lot happier.

In this interchange, Margaret expresses a key emergent meaning-making marker of an untold story when she asks the therapist, "I don't know whether it is good to go back like this or not; is it?" With the expression of the untold story meaning-making marker, Margaret sought out and received reassurance from her therapist (i.e., "I think it is") that (a) returning to painful memories of past events is of key importance for understanding where her current problematic emotions "come from" and (b) her feelings of resentment and anger toward her husband are of importance and point to a personally salient experience that has not yet been fully storied or understood.

Her therapist's response, "I think it is, because it sounds like you're still holding feelings from back then," demonstrates a keen attunement to the emergent meaning potential of Margaret's untold story. Margaret is in agreement with her therapist and the importance of addressing painful emotional memories when she states, "If I could just let go of some of these feelings, I think I would be an awful lot happier." After receiving reassurance from her therapist that disclosing troubling emotional memories is important for how therapy "works," Margaret recalls the point in time (i.e., the year when everything seemed to happen) when she first started to feel tensions in her marriage and a growing estrangement from her husband. It is in the context of a secure therapeutic bond with strong agreement on tasks and goals that she discloses a highly distressing emotional memory (i.e., an untold story) that happened during "that year":

> Yeah, it really, it was very bad. I was spending more and more time at over there (at my parents' apartment) and of course then I think there was the resentment too of—I come from a fairly big family; like, I have two sisters and three brothers—but I was doing all the work. Like, I was over cleaning the apartment and making meals and they started getting, like, particularly my Dad started getting terribly confused.

Margaret then moves to a reflexive meaning-making stance to provide an overall assessment of that time in her life (i.e., "It really was horrendous") and then, spontaneously, a specific new emotional awareness emerges for Margaret in the sessions: "And I think [takes a deep breath] the part that hurt the most [starts crying] was that . . . it was my mother's reaction to me. At times, you know [crying], it would really hurt."

It is in the context of this new emotional experience that Margaret discloses a specific, detailed ABM of her mother that provides a narrative context for her acute feelings of hurt:

> One time in the apartment they got cockroaches. Oh, and of course I had to go over, and my mother—all my life I, my mother was the fussiest

housekeeper; I mean she kept her house immaculate—and, um, I had to go over and empty out all the cupboards for them to come in and spray. I mean, it was just horrible—you know—they and, I mean, I, I figured I kept the apartment as clean as I could possibly clean it, but, um, as I say, this time with the cockroaches. So, I went over the night before, I emptied all the cupboards, and my mother [sighs]—it was just horrendous—saying "I don't have cockroaches; it's only dirty people that have those." And, oh, she just went on and on and on and on. And she went down the hall to the superintendent's door—and I was in the apartment when it was happening [sniffs]—and she was telling them that I was forcing her to do this, that sort of thing. And then I went in the elevator to try and bring her back upstairs again. She hit me, and [crying] I think that was the most horrible thing—you know—to stand there in that elevator and your mother hits you, at my age?

In terms of indicators of narrative change, in contrast to Margaret's overgeneral recounting of her empty story of depression in Session 1 and her same old story accounts, the disclosure of her mother's assault in Session 11 is highly specific and emotion charged. The disclosure of this painful, previously untold story is the starting point for addressing the broken story that is at the core of her depression.

As described in Chapter 4, when clients recall emotionally traumatizing memories, painful, disturbing emotions may resist assimilation to preexisting views and beliefs about self and others, which is definitive of a broken story (emotional incoherence subtype). Especially in the context of a child's relationship with his or her parents, unexpected breaches of safety and trust may also call into question the loving intentions of the other. In addition, primary maladaptive emotions such as feelings of humiliation, disgust, shame, and/or fear are often accompanied by a withdrawal from others (Greenberg, 2002) that further impedes the disclosure of the distressing experiences to friends or family. Finally, a further sense of betrayal, isolation, anger, and resentment may ensue if attempts to tell others about the emotionally distressing experience are minimized, ignored, or rebuffed.

To help Margaret more fully differentiate the painful emotions evoked by her experiences with her mother and acknowledge their full impact on her life, the therapist poses the following question.

Therapist: I wonder if you really ever have allowed yourself to realize how awful it was?

Client: I think what you said is really true; people would say, "Oh, it must have been horrible," and I think, huh, it wasn't that bad [flippantly], but then, maybe my mind's just shutting it out because it was horrible. Because when I think, like, that situation, when my mother hit me? [becomes tearful] It was almost like, um, I'm so ashamed, you know that?

As noted in Chapter 5, to heighten the experiential impact of an empathic reflection, it is helpful to differentiate the feeling in the context of the original event. Margaret's therapist skillfully demonstrates how to do this when she combines the narrative action of the scene (i.e., "Here she is hitting you") with Margaret's internal world of emotions and intentions (i.e., "And you're trying to do what's best for her") in response to Margaret's disclosure of feeling shame. This empathic response evocatively highlights the disjunction between Margaret's caring intentions and the angry assault she experiences at the hands of her confused mother. It is precisely the confusing disjunction between good intentions and unexpected bad outcomes, along with conflicting feelings of anger, shame, and humiliation, that are key characteristics of broken story markers and which may have contributed to Margaret "shutting out" her own emotional experiences of that "horrible" year that results in the sense of feeling stuck in a confusing, puzzling story that resists understanding and integration.

The third stage thus involves an emotional transformation and the enactment of a new story outcome based on Margaret changing her basic mode of emotional responding from shame to allowing herself to feel hurt by her mother's actions and feeling some anger at being wronged. Her shift from primary maladaptive withdrawal emotions of fear and shame in relation to the traumatic event to her primary adaptive approach emotions of anger and sadness helped her restore her self-esteem and promoted grieving for what was lost. This promoted the narrative change. Margaret's change occurred because her shame and fear—and the narrative meanings they conveyed—were transformed into sadness and anger.

Phase 4: Self-Narrative Reflection and Reconstruction

Margaret's and the therapist's reflections on the meanings and feelings involved in her previously unprocessed broken story lead her to a major change in narrative trajectory. As she reflects on the broken story, a clear beginning, middle, and end emerge, with actions coherently organized along an unfolding time line. Margaret includes in her new narrative an integrated representation of the intentions, emotions, and perceptions she experienced in the context of the unfolding action.

From her own perspective, Margaret had felt terribly let down by her husband's failure to provide her with the emotional support that she had felt she wanted, needed, and deserved at that moment in her life. It is in the context of exploring the full emotional impact of the distressing memory of her mother's assault, and in response to her therapist's evocative empathic response, that Margaret suddenly experiences a new appreciation of her husband's actions and the intentions that may have been behind them during "that horrible year." In essence, Margaret experiences a moment of new emotional awareness that emerges from the heightened narrative contextualization of that terrible year:

> And, but, you know, to give Carl credit, and I guess I have blamed him for this, but, actually, I guess, in a way to give him credit, he has never brought that up to me, the confusion that it cost with our family. He has never once referred to it.

It is at this moment that Margaret begins to reevaluate whether Carl's seeming lack of interest in her past family troubles might actually have arisen out of caring intentions and a desire to protect her from having to remember what really happened. Margaret recalls the following memory:

> He used to get mad at my sisters; he would get furious, and then it got to the point that—I wouldn't, if I were mad, was mad at them—I wouldn't say anything to Carl because I know—you know—and then I'd say to him, "Don't you dare talk about my sisters like that!" So, it got to the point that he said nothing, and then it got to the point that I withdrew even more because he wouldn't say anything against my sisters. So, and I wouldn't get any action from him, so I just didn't talk about it.

Margaret's disclosure of this generic ABM narrative provides a new, more comprehensive account of the respective roles that both partners played in the inception of the communication rupture in their marriage. Elaborating Margaret's subjective feelings and needs, the therapist offers the following empathic conjecture: "So somehow you wanted support, and yet, what he—when he said something and it was against your family, it kind of hurt you and so you kind of pushed him away a bit."

Continuing to reflect on her experiences with Carl, and in light of her therapist's articulation of a new, more coherent emotional plotline, Margaret begins to consider for the first time that she may have had a part to play in her husband's emotional withdrawal from her, and she begins to shift from anger to the beginnings of compassion and empathy for her husband: "I mean, as I say, I'll admit, like, it really was a bad time, and as I say, part of it was my fault too; I guess maybe I pushed Carl away in a lot of ways." This idea sets the stage for a new, more compassionate understanding of Carl's feelings and concerns: "So that he got to the point, he thought OK, that's the way she feels, she can—I'm not gonna, you know, try any more."

In the context of this extended, reflexive inquiry, a new emotional experience and a moment of insight occur for Margaret:

> Maybe Carl felt—I never thought about it this way until now—but maybe he felt so left out too, maybe he just felt left out. You know, I have never

looked at it this way before; isn't that strange. I just had this feeling of resentment that my sole support wasn't there, and maybe he just felt left out—you know—that, as I say, I was so consumed with my parents—so angry, so let down—that maybe I pushed him out of my life.

In this moment of emotional insight, Margaret begins to challenge her own belief that her husband abandoned her emotionally in a time of acute distress and starts to consider the new emotional plotline that he may have in fact felt "pushed out" by her anger, her feelings of resentment toward her siblings, and her own emotional withdrawal in the face of painful memories of humiliation and shame. She feels more caring for him, which helps transform her resentment.

Moreover, in addition to resolving the emotional incoherence of Margaret's broken story of her marriage, the therapist also helps her to coconstruct a new, more coherent narrative account that addresses the genesis or "cause" of her feelings of resentment toward Carl by linking her current feelings of anger and resentment with past hurtful and shame-filled encounters with her disabled parents. In essence, Margaret's shift in the therapy session from experiencing anger and frustration (secondary emotions) to an awareness of hurt (primary emotions) and shame (primary maladaptive emotion) represents a new emotional plotline that leads to new ways of seeing and experiencing what happened with her parents and her husband. In this reconstructed narrative, the therapist identifies Margaret's powerful feelings of hurt and shame felt in relation to her mother as preceding and setting the stage for her strong feelings of resentment and anger toward her husband, followed eventually by some compassion for him: "It is important to remember how tough it was back then, and maybe some of those feelings spilled over to the marriage when, really, a lot of the turmoil was from other things."

In terms of story reconstruction, Margaret begins to feel more compassion for her husband and realizes that some of her own actions may have contributed to the problems in her marriage and that she may be able to change her behavior to secure better outcomes in the future. In addition, in the presence of a caring and skilled therapist she has received strong validation for the expression of her painful emotions and need for nurturance and care. Margaret may now be willing to see whether those needs might be seriously addressed in the context of her relationship with her husband.

CONCLUSION

Margaret's active reflective awareness of her own intense emotional distress in the context of an emotionally charged, specific memory narrative sets the stage for the emergence of a new, more compassionate understanding of her husband's intentions and actions in relation to her own unmet needs. Her new interpersonal insight specifically addressed the narrative coherence of her story of depression wherein her husband's hurtful actions are now understood as unintended outcomes of caring intentions. Margaret develops a new appreciation of her own emotional needs and the role she may have played in the development of a communication breakdown with her husband. As such, she gains a new appreciation of her own agency and the hopeful possibility that she may be able to make a positive difference in her marriage.

At the same time, it is clear that the therapist's empathic validation of the importance of disclosing past memories set the stage for Margaret's emotional disclosure about her mother. In addition, it was the therapist's responsive empathic attunement to Margaret's emotional experiencing in the context of the specific ABM disclosure that helped Margaret organize and contain previously avoided feelings of hurt, fear, and shame that were evoked by the recounting of the remembered event. In addition, the therapist's empathic attunement to Margaret's affective processes in the context of her ABM disclosure helped Margaret assimilate warded-off affects that, when reintegrated, altered the essential meaning of her story. Although the events of the story remain intact, it is the emotional meanings of actions taken by self and others that have changed. The therapist's sustained empathic engagement with her in the context of a caring therapeutic relationship is a lived instantiation of the possibility of achieving that goal and may constitute a corrective relational experience of therapy.

7

WORKING WITH NARRATIVE AND EMOTION IN TRAUMA: THE CASE OF ALEX

In this chapter we present the intensive case analysis of one good outcome, brief emotion-focused therapy (EFT) dyad (Angus & Bouffard, 2004) drawn from the York Unfinished Business Study (Greenberg & Malcolm, 2002; Paivio & Greenberg, 1995). The client, named Alexandra for the purpose of this chapter, brings to life her previously untold story of the traumatic loss of her mother by suicide and, together with her EFT therapist, reauthors a new account of the broken story that has plagued her for more than 20 years. To illuminate four stages of narrative-emotion integration in EFT, key episodes are drawn from therapy sessions to illustrate how EFT therapists facilitate emotion and narrative coherence when working with emotional trauma. This chapter begins with an overview of emotional trauma from a narrative-emotion perspective, followed by an overview of treating broken stories, the predominant problem marker emerging in this case study. Then, we discuss the four phases of treatment for this case.

OVERVIEW OF EMOTIONAL TRAUMA FROM A NARRATIVE-EMOTIONAL PERSPECTIVE

For EFT therapists, broken stories represent that subset of client concerns that develop as a result of conflictual and/or traumatic interactions with significant others that result in a profound sense of narrative and/or emotional incoherence. A defining characteristic of a trauma-based broken story is the feeling of being trapped in an emotionally exhausting, unresolvable dilemma. On the one hand, there is an urgent desire to rid the self completely of the traumatic memory that disrupts the emotional plotlines of one's life and to avoid the painful emotions that are connected to the experience. On the other hand, an array of ordinary, everyday experiences inexplicably cue memories of the trauma and/or unbidden emotions, such as fear, rage, sadness, and anger, that evoke maladaptive emotional schemes and are residues of the trauma.

In addition, there is often a nagging awareness that to achieve closure, the circumstances of the traumatic situation, or sets of experiences, must be reengaged in such a way that an understandable, emotionally coherent and livable account of both the event and its aftermath can be constructed and integrated into the sense of self and life story. It is this quest for coherence and understanding that propels trauma survivors to tell and retell their story over and over again to anyone who will listen. The emergence of a coherent trauma narrative enables trauma survivors to reflexively "look back on" the trauma experience and, from this new vantage point, begin to construct a more comprehensive and emotionally coherent understanding of what happened and what it means in terms of views of self and others. And perhaps most important, the telling of trauma tales also elicits the support and concerns of others and reinstates a sense of personal safety and connection with caring others, enhancing attachment relationships.

Conversely, when there is no community of support or when the trauma stories are forbidden to be retold—as is sometimes the situation in cases of sexual assault and parental suicide in childhood—distressing emotions remain "raw," unintegrated, and disruptively active in the person's ongoing life (Paivio & Pascual-Leone, 2010). From a narrative perspective, trauma-related unfinished business is a type of broken story and emotional incoherence in which the client's thoughts and feelings about the traumatic event have remained fragmented, disconnected, and "not understood." It is in this manner that traumatic memories of loss resist assimilation into preexisting views of self and others in the world. As noted previously, there needs to be a match between the emotions felt and the intentions attributed to actions undertaken in a situation to generate a coherent memory narrative of a lived experience. In the case of trauma-related memories, the overpowering, and at times contradictory, emotions experienced in relation to the devastating events resist assimilation into preexisting story structures.

For instance, when a child suffers the suicide of a parent, the question of who is responsible for the horrific loss is of paramount importance. The motivations and actions of self and others are called into question. Basic attachment needs for safe and trustworthy care are shattered, and a sense of deep betrayal, as well as profound grief and loss, may persist for years after the loss of the significant other. Emotional memories of the trauma scene are disjunctive with preexisting attachment-related emotion schemes and exert a disorganizing influence on the sense of self, pre- and posttrauma. It is as if a sudden disconnect occurs between the child who existed prior to the suicide and the one who emerges from the devastating loss and has to find a way to go on living. Hence, in the context of working with clients who are stuck in a broken story in response to sudden, traumatic loss, it is not only the trauma memory but also the lifelong emotional impact of that loss that must be acknowledged, storied, and understood. Long-standing feelings of resentment, bitterness, anger, and shame may permeate the stories told about the deceased parent and reflect the deep sense of betrayal felt by the survivor self.

To illuminate the four stages of narrative-emotion change in EFT, key episodes were drawn from the transcribed therapy sessions of one good outcome EFT dyad from the York Unfinished Business Study (Greenberg & Malcolm, 2002; Paivio & Greenberg, 1995). The client, Alexandra, was 12 years old when her mother killed herself by shotgun blast. A suicide note gave no specific reason for her decision to take her life. Alex was the first person to discover her mother at the time of her suicide and exhibited symptoms of posttraumatic stress disorder at pretreatment assessment. The client was 35 years old when she presented for treatment and stated, "I would like to find a better way of accepting myself and being OK with myself." She reported chronic feelings of anxiety, insecurity, and shame, despite a successful business career and stable marriage. Alex also reported strong feelings of anger and resentment toward her mother, 20 years after her death. She found it difficult to live with the shameful secret of her mother's suicide and was unable to tell others about the circumstances of her death. Alex completed 15 sessions of EFT for unfinished business at the York Psychotherapy Clinic.

At posttreatment assessment, Alex's pretreatment Symptom Checklist-90-Revised (SCL-90-R; Derogatis, Rickels, & Rock, 1976) score of 81 dropped to 35. On postsession self-report measures she identified herself as having experienced significant change in relation to key concerns and stated that she had achieved a sense of resolution with her mother at therapy termination. The therapist who worked with Alex was an advanced clinical psychology doctoral student in her late 30s who had 3 years of clinical experience and 1 year of supervised training in EFT.

We now describe how the goal of narrative and emotion integration—repairing a broken story—was addressed in the context of Alex's courageous struggle to understand and accept the traumatic loss of her mother.

OVERVIEW OF TREATMENT: REPAIRING BROKEN STORIES

We use the term *broken stories* to signify when clients experience an unexpected disruption to the narrative trajectory of a desired life plan, which results in a confusing array of feelings that may include hurt, sadness, anger, resentment, and shame. We have found that the process of facilitating emotion and narrative integration for the repair of client broken stories is greatly facilitated by the use of imaginal role-plays during therapy sessions, particularly the empty-chair technique.

When using this intervention, EFT therapists follow an empathic style and, having established an alliance, introduce an empty-chair dialogue when they detect a marker of unfinished business. Such markers typically involve the client giving expression to lingering unresolved feelings toward a significant other, or statements of painful childhood memories. Nonverbal behavior, such as stifling tears or holding one's breath, and/or interrupted or restricted expressions of anger over past treatment often accompany these moments in therapy sessions. A vital element in this process of engaging in lively contact with the imagined other is that creative adjustment is facilitated by the restorying of the person's emotional memories and by the emergence of new views of self and significant others. Emotional arousal is viewed as a key mechanism in evoking salient memories and accessing self–other schematic structures (Greenberg & Malcolm, 2002).

The use of empty chair in EFT for trauma facilitates in three important ways the client's reengagement in emotions evoked in the context of his or her memory of the traumatic event and the negative life consequences that followed. First, to address broken stories in which the narrative coherence has been disrupted, the EFT therapist helps the client to access, disclose, and externalize lived experiences of loss and trauma (i.e., untold stories markers) for the development of a coherent narrative account that articulates an unfolding plotline that now has a beginning, middle, and end. The therapist's capacity to empathically attend to the client's key concerns in the context of recounting the trauma event is essential for the development of a strong therapeutic alliance and basic trust in the therapist. The narrative contextualization of trauma experiences as told stories enables both client and therapist to undertake a reflective exploration of the emotional meaning of the event for the client.

Next, the client is helped to contextualize and integrate painful emotions in the context of the traumatic memory of the suicide event. The differentiation and narrative organization of painful emotion enables the client to reflexively explore and symbolize emergent meanings of the trauma and loss from a variety of relational vantage points. For example, the first vantage point that emerged for Alex in her therapy sessions was the perspective and story of the "traumatized child." It was the 12-year-old Alex who was the first to discover her dead mother's body at the time of her suicide. The second vantage point addressed in the therapy sessions was that of the adult "survivor self" who managed to find a way to live in loss and who emerged after her mother's death. Angus and Bouffard-Bowes (2002) addressed the voice and story of the survivor self.

Finally, in response to telling her story, the vantage point of the lost mother then emerged and became a focus in the therapy sessions. Alex was encouraged to place an imaginal representation of her mother in the empty chair and to voice her mother's response to Alex's stories of loss and unrelenting emotional pain. This facilitated the emergence of the mother's story and her affirmation of her enduring love for her children and her profound remorse and regret for the impact that her suicide has had on her children. In this dialogue the client also voiced the mother's suicide story and explored her mother's possible intentions and beliefs at the time of the suicide.

PHASE 1: BONDING, NARRATIVE UNFOLDING, AND AWARENESS

First of all, the EFT therapist helps the client to access and disclose the untold story of the trauma event—for narrative reorganization and emotion narrative integration—by being an empathic, supportive, and trustworthy listener. The experience of being heard by a trustworthy and empathic listener encourages the client to express and story painful emotions and validates the importance of the client's quest for understanding, self-acceptance, and where possible, forgiveness.

For Alex, the opportunity to tell her story was particularly important because she and her siblings had been advised by extended family members to not talk about her mother's death with anyone. Her mother's death was experienced as a painful, shameful family secret that was best left untold. During the third therapy session, addressing her mother in the empty chair, Alex disclosed the following autobiographical memory (ABM) that meets criteria for an untold story marker:

> We never talked about you after you died. It was just kind of—it was just there. Dad never talked about you, although he missed you very much. It was very painful for me to listen to him crying for you in his sleep and crying for you and crying because he felt so bad that you did what you . . . [*Therapist:* Hmm.] He didn't—I don't know if he knew why you did what

you did—he never talked about it. I don't think he knew. He went on a road to, on a road of self-destruction to kill himself. It took him 10 years after you died for him to do it, but he did finally accomplished that too.

When the therapist acknowledged the enormity of the loss of both her mother and father, Alex disclosed, "I don't think I've ever had the privilege of even being able to accept that—even within my family—the loss. It was just supposed to be that things went on merrily after." Her confirmation that she had never had an opportunity to tell her story of trauma and loss (i.e., an untold story marker) lays the ground for the intensive exploration of the trauma event and the description of both what happened and how Alex experienced it.

The suicide of a parent is a highly traumatizing experience, especially during childhood. To construct a meaningful, coherent understanding of "what happened," Alex first needed to story the horrifying childhood experience of discovering her dead mother and to distinguish that experience from the devastating emotional impact that ensued after her suicide. With the sudden and unexpected death of a parent, children experience overwhelming feelings of grief and sadness, fears of abandonment, and a profound breach of trust or betrayal of the safety, fairness, and goodness of the world. Moreover, childhood survivors of suicide are left to question why the parent chose to abandon them.

In response to her therapist's empathic support, Alex begins to disclose her painful memories of finding her mother shortly after she had committed suicide in the family home. In the following sequences the therapist empathically supports the client in disclosing her traumatic untold story by guiding her to (a) provide a detailed unfolding of the sequence of events that frame the suicide scene for heightened narrative coherence and (b) differentiate specific emotions, intentions, and appraisals experienced in the context of the scene for heightened emotional coherence.

Client: I just can't—you know—because the images of certain things like that are so clear in my mind and it was so long ago. And I said that to my sister yesterday, that night is so clear to me.

Therapist: The night she died.

Client: The night she killed herself. It's so clear; I can remember everything.

Therapist: Just like it happened yesterday.

Client: And I remember and it sort of came into clear focus of me as a kid, and I hate it, I mean, I hate it [emotional differentiation]. I remember the night that my mother died, that's what it was like [emergence of single event memory of suicide scene]. I was walking and my brother and sister—my sister was supposed to be babysitting my brother in the house—

and, um, it was quiet and I thought they were waiting to jump out and go "Boo!" You know? Kids' stuff. [*Therapist:* Mm-hmm.] So I tiptoe, tiptoe up the sidewalk and open the front door very carefully and listen: still nothing, just the sound in my eardrums [experiential awareness].

Therapist: This deafening silence [therapist empathic evocative reflection].

Client: So quiet, and I'm thinking this is really berserk, really crazy, because usually by now they've jumped out and scared the living daylights out of me, and we've all laughed. [*Therapist:* Mm-hmm.] And punched each other or whatever kids do. And I remember walking in and still nothing and thinking this is really funny, and I took my boots off and I went creeping down into kitchen and I saw my mother's foot first and I was in absolute shock and not knowing what to do.

Therapist: And your heart almost stopped.

Client: And I started shouting because I thought my sister was supposed to be there, and I started screaming for my sister, and then I noticed that on the table there was a note saying that she was over at my aunt's and uncle's at a New Year's party, and they had put my little brother to bed there and that was really because of all the turmoil as a child too I was frightened to call anybody because you know your own business stays within the four walls of your house so . . .

Therapist: Sure, sure.

Client: It felt like 10 hours. I'm sure it was a minute, but it seemed like 10 hours.

Therapist: So, then you walked in and saw what had actually happened [therapist invites a return to elaboration of unfolding plotline for heightened narrative coherence].

Client: I tried waking her up. I thought she might just have—you know . . .

Therapist: Who knows as a child?

Client: And I'm just shaking her and shaking her and trying to wake her up and thinking—you know—oh, God, what do I do? Who do I call? What do I do? [*Therapist:* Mmm.] So, the first thing I did, I called my uncle and he came over with my sister because of course I said—I don't know what I said, I have no idea—and of course when he came in, my heart also goes out to him because I can't imagine an adult—myself—now walking in on a situation like that—with your family.

In this sequence, both the client and the therapist collaborate in a detailed unfolding of the trauma scene in the context of a narrative framework with a clear beginning, middle, and end. In addition, a clear scene and setting is provided along with the internal experiences of both the protagonist (Alex) and significant others involved in the event (the uncle). For the first time, a coherent narrative of the trauma memory—an untold story—begins to take shape for Alex. In addition, both client and therapist contribute to a coelaboration of emotions, intentions, and expectations in the context of the unfolding narrative scene that Alex experienced at the time of her mother's suicide.

PHASE 2: EVOCATION AND ARTICULATION OF NARRATIVE THEMES

In the following example of an empty-chair intervention in Session 7, the therapist first invites Alex to describe the trauma scene, then encourages her to elaborate felt emotions. The client moves back and forth between describing the remembered suicidal scene and describing her felt emotions in response to these terrifying images. In this therapeutic dance, the therapist empathically follows the client's lead and facilitates the expression of painful emotions and deep fears that are now contextualized within the unfolding narrative plotline of the trauma story. Finally, the client shifts to a reflective questioning mode at the end of the sequence, in an attempt to bring understanding to this trauma experience.

Therapist: Tell her what you remember about the things, about the memories [therapist invites client narrative disclosure].

Client: The horror and the terror [tearfully; client focuses on felt emotions].

Therapist: Let it go [therapist stays with the client focus on felt emotions and differentiates fear, horror, and terror]. Tell her about your fear [client takes a tissue], the horror, and the terror [pauses]. Stay with it; you're doing well. What do you remember? Tell her what it's like for you. It's important.

Client: [Crying] I feel these memories are absolutely horrific and things I never should have seen.

Therapist: Tell her.

Client: It's etched so deeply in my mind, I can't erase it. When I think of you, I can't even think of you because I just remember you . . .

Therapist: Tell her what you see [therapist invites a shift back to trauma scene].

Client: All I see is just you laying there. I can't believe it, and you're not waking . . .

Therapist: Not waking up. What's it like for you? [Invites client to elaborate lived experience.]

Client: I'm just so afraid. [Client shift to internal emotional differentiation.]

Therapist: I feel terrified. [Therapist empathic reflection and emotional differentiation.] That's good; keep breathing. I feel terrified. What's going on? [Therapist's question invites the client to differentiate emotional experiencing further.]

Client: And absolute disbelief. How could you, how could you?

Therapist: So, how could you do this? [Therapist invites client to confront her mother directly with her reflexive questions in a search for understanding and meaning.] Tell her this.

Client: I don't really understand why you did it.

Therapist: Stay with those memories. And what do you want to say? [Client pauses.] What are you feeling now? [Therapist invites client to elaborate felt emotion.]

Client: [Pauses; client continues in reflexive narrative mode.] I'm thinking that, um, how can I, how can something that happened so long ago control me so much now?

It is important to note that in Session 7, after this disclosure of her trauma, Alex returned to the suicide scene on several other occasions in later sessions. It was as if her vantage point on the suicide scene shifted and changed over time, with new meanings emerging in each retelling. In particular, the back-and-forth movement between the vantage point of the traumatized child caught in the unfolding suicide scenario and the adult survivor self who is resentful and bitter about her mother's actions seemed to be an important aspect of articulating and integrating the meaning of emotions, appraisals, and beliefs across time and settings.

PHASE 3: EMOTIONAL TRANSFORMATION AND NEW STORY OUTCOMES

The narrative-informed EFT model of resolution of unfinished business suggests that in the context of repairing broken stories, a client's repetitive expression of needing to know "why" a hurtful action was undertaken is almost always a marker of underlying feelings of resentment and hurt. From this perspective, it is argued that negative feelings need to be openly expressed and responded to by the significant other so that successful problem resolution—and a positive emotional shift—can take place. Having developed a differentiated, emotionally coherent narrative account of her mother's suicide and having acknowledged her sadness because of her loss and clearly symbolized her needs for security and relief, Alex can now reflexively distance herself from the emotional pain of the hurt child and enter into the world of the distressed other, her mother. For the first time, Alex is able to imaginatively enter into her mother's "inner world" and begin to articulate her probable motives, emotions, beliefs, thoughts, and intentions at the time of the suicide. The reflexive reprocessing of emotion-laden traumatic memories, as seen through the eyes of the other, facilitates the creation of new meanings and a more emotionally coherent account of the traumatic loss, which addresses the dual perspectives of Alex and her mother in relation to her mother's suicide.

Mother, role-played by Alex in the context of empty-chair dialogues, now has an opportunity to (a) provide an account of personal responsibility for the suicide and clarify her intentions for committing suicide, (b) acknowledge responsibility for the loss and devastation that ensued after her death and express deep regret for the unforeseen and unintended impact on her children's lives, and most important, (c) affirm her love for the client. In the following empty-chair dialogue, all three critical issues are powerfully addressed in the context of the client's expression of puzzlement—a client process key marker of a broken story subtype, emotional incoherence—regarding her mother's reasons for committing suicide. In the position of her mother, in the empty chair, Alex gives voice to the following account in which she provides a differentiated account of her suicidal intentions and motives and asks her daughter for forgiveness.

Client: Yes, I wasn't well and I didn't mean to hurt you children. [Elaboration of the meaning of the mother's suicidal intentions and motives.] I didn't know the kind of impact it would have on you. I obviously didn't think about it very much. I should have gone for help, you're right. I should have gone to my—I had, I have a large family—I should have gone to my brothers and sisters for help. I should have made sure you kids were taken care of. I should have done a lot of things that I didn't do.

Therapist: So, I made a terrible mistake. [Therapist meaning coconstruction]

Client: I made a terrible mistake. [The client, role-playing the mother, restates her new admission that the suicide was a mistake—an error in judgment—that she wishes she had not made and elaborates the meaning of this new realization in

Therapist: Sounds like "I'm sorry."

Client: I can't undo it and I'm very sorry for hurting you. [From her mother's perspective, the client articulates her regrets about the hurtful impact of her suicide on her daughter.]

Therapist: Can you say that again?

Client: I'm very, very sorry for hurting you. I'm not there now, and I'm really sorry for the things that you feel that I've done to you . . . [a new perspective on the mother's caring for her children emerges in the context of her personal account of the circumstances or reasons why she made a terrible mistake and committed suicide] wasn't about you kids at all. You're probably the reason that I stayed as long as I did stay. It wasn't about you children. It was about a life that I just thought there was no hope and a sense of hopelessness.

This affirmation of enduring love from her mother sets the stage for Alex to address the question of her mother's intentions at the time of the suicide. This inquiry is undertaken from the perspective of a loved child who is trying to understand how and under what conditions a caring mother can commit such a tragic mistake without knowing that it will have devastating emotional outcomes for family and loved ones. It is important that the mother provide a compelling account that not only includes the circumstances that led to her suicide, and her motivation and intentions for doing so, but also expresses her deep remorse for her actions and her recognition of and responsibility for the devastating impact it had on others.

Later in the same session, a significant shift occurs when Alex, role-playing her mother, articulates a new, more integrative account of the mother's suicide story in which she now acknowledges that her suicide was based on a mistaken belief of not being cared for by others, and she expresses her deep regret for her actions and affirms her continuing love for her children. The following dialogue also occurred in Session 9.

Client: I am so very, very sorry that I did what I did to you. And you're right, I didn't realize the ripple effect of what I did to your father and to your brother, your sister, my own sisters, and my own parents even. I, I saw the pain. There was no turning back at that point; I had already done what I had done. And I never realized for a moment, until the aftermath,

>
> that there was so many people that cared about me as much as they did care about me. And I did have alternatives and I did have places to go. [*Therapist:* Mmm.] I didn't exercise those options. I don't know why I didn't exercise them, but it was too late to exercise them.

Therapist: Mmm. "I need you to forgive. I'm sorry for what I did. I need you to forgive me."

Client: I cared about you children more than anything in the whole world. I can't make an excuse for what I did. I've no—I don't know why, it just was there. But I should not have left you children. I love you more than anything in the world and it's been very difficult for the three of you all of these years. [*Therapist:* Hmm.] And I never should have left you.

The question of whether a mother who loves her children can commit suicide is reengaged from a new perspective in which the parent has now expressed profound regrets regarding her selfish actions, a wish to undo her actions if she could, and enduring love for her children. This invites a compassionate understanding of the mother's distress from the perspective of the traumatized child and opens up the possibility of forgiveness. It is not until Session 11, however, that the client, role-playing her mother, takes responsibility for all of the painful consequences of her suicide, expresses deep remorse for her thoughtless actions, and asks Alex for forgiveness.

Client: [Softly] I, I wish there was something that I could do to change it, what I did, to undo what I did. You're making me understand the devastation that I caused and the aftermath. It wasn't just about me, it was about a lot of other people. [Pauses, voice breaking] I really wish that you could forgive me. I know . . .

Therapist: Say this again: "I really need you to forgive me."

Client: [Voice breaking and crying] I really need, I really need you to forgive me. I know that you've struggled all of your life dealing with something that's [crying], that was my problem, and that's very unfair.

Therapist: That's unfair.

Client: [Crying] Definitely. I'm sorry.

Therapist: "It's my fault, and I'm sorry."

Client: [Crying] I never should have done what I did.

Therapist: Hmm, that wasn't an answer.

Therapist: [Softly] It was a big mistake.

Client: It was a really big mistake. I never should have done that. There were other alternatives. I didn't need to do this.

Therapist: Hmm.

Client: [Crying] I hope that you can find some inner peace.

Therapist: Hmm. Tell her what would be so important about forgiving, why you need her forgiveness.

Client: I need you to forgive me because most importantly, it's [sighing; pauses] . . . I do have to get on. I can't, I, I realize that this has burdened you all of your life and by forgiving me you will release yourself of the pain [crying].

Therapist: Hmm, so, "I don't want to burden you anymore."

Client: [Crying] I want you to be able to be rid of me. I want you to be able to have good memories of me and to let me go and to not have those bad memories. I want you, when you think of me, to think of somebody who wasn't well and who did violate you and your father and your brother and your sister.

Therapist: So, "I want you to know I wasn't well."

Client: Yeah, I really wasn't well. I didn't know what was going on, and I just felt that I had no place to turn. I was full of despair.

Therapist: Just full of despair.

Client: And there wasn't an alternative.

Therapist: Hmm, "I wish I could undo it. I can't undo it." What do you want her to know?

Client: I cared about you children more than anything in the whole world. I can't make an excuse for what I did. I've no . . . I don't know why, it just was there, but I should not have left you children. I love you more than anything in the world and it's been very difficult for the three of you all of these years, and I never should have left you, and if I needed help I should have made sure that there was someone else that could have helped us, you. I shouldn't have just left you.

Therapist: "I shouldn't have just left you."

Client: I never should have abandoned you.

Therapist: "I shouldn't. I'm sorry I abandoned you."

Client: It was wrong.

Therapist: It was wrong. Say that again: "It was wrong."

Client: It was wrong. You were my responsibility and your father's responsibility and it was wrong of me to leave you. I was in control of that; you were children. [*Therapist:* Hmm.] I should have dealt with it and I didn't.

Therapist: "And I'm sorry."

Client: And I am sorry. I'm sorry.

Therapist: Can you tell her again that it wasn't you?

Client: This wasn't . . . my suicide wasn't about you kids at all. You're probably the reason that I stayed as long as I did stay. It wasn't about you children. It was about a life that I just thought there was no hope and a sense of hopelessness. I need you to understand that it isn't about you. It really isn't about you. I did love you. I do love you. I do love your brother and your sister. It's not about anything that you did. You're not responsible for what I did. Your father wasn't responsible for what I did. I'm responsible for what I did. I am responsible [crying].

In the context of her poignant plea for forgiveness, "Alex's mother" also articulates a new, more compassionate retelling of her suicide story in which she now takes responsibility for the consequences of her actions that occurred at a point in her life in which she was experiencing a desperate sense of hopelessness. This is the story of a loving mother who makes a tragic decision to take her own life while caught in the grip of despair and depression. It is in response to her mother's new compelling account that Alex expresses forgiveness to her mother for the first time.

Therapist: Can you come over here? [Client changes chairs.] What happens to you hearing that?

Client: [Pauses] I think, I think Mom, I think for the first time I'm starting to, I want to forgive you. And, uh, I've always wanted to forgive you. I [pauses], I think, I, I, I do forgive you, Mom.

Therapist: Can you say that again: "I do forgive you"?

Client: [Crying] I forgive you, Mom.

Therapist: Again?

Client: I forgive you, Mom.

Therapist: What happens as you say that?

Client: [Crying] It's, oh I think that with the forgiveness, I lose it, I lose her.

Therapist: Can you say, "I'm afraid of losing you"?

Client: I'm afraid that through the forgiveness that I would lose you. [Crying] I don't know what I'm hanging on to. I feel that with the forgiveness, you're gone. And I feel sad [crying].

Therapist: "I feel sad that you're gone. I don't want to let you go." [Sound of client blowing her nose] Hmm, hmm.

Client: I'm really sad that you're gone.

Therapist: Can you tell her about that . . . hanging on, not wanting to let her go?

Client: I don't want to hang on to the negative. I want to hang on to the positive. I really don't want to forget you. I loved you very much as a child and I love you very much now [voice breaking and crying].

Therapist: "And I don't want to forget you."

Client: I don't want to forget you, but I want to, I want to feel comforting when I think of you. I don't want to feel turmoil and aggravation and that responsibility. [Crying] I want to feel good. I want to feel warm when I think about you. I don't want to feel chilly and cold and upset. I want to think of you in a nice way.

Therapist: Hmm, so, "I need the happy, comforting part of you to stay with me."

Client: Yes. [Blows her nose.]

Therapist: Can you come over here? [Client changes chairs.] What does she say? "I'm afraid of losing you completely; I need the comforting parts."

Client: [Crying] I love you, Alex, and I won't leave you. I want you to think about the times that you do think about as a child, when you did feel loved, because you do, you were loved. It's not your imagination or your perception: You were loved; you were genuinely loved.

Therapist: Hmm, "I genuinely loved you."

Client: And I need you to focus and to think of me in those terms. I made a terrible mistake and by forgiving me for my mistake and thinking about the good things and the good times—the laughing—and I need you to remember me like that. Because that was really me, Alex. The other side you know, that wasn't me.

Therapist: Hmm, "That was really me, all that love."

Client: All, all that caring and nurturing for you when you were a small child.

PHASE 4: SELF-NARRATIVE REFLECTION AND RECONSTRUCTION

The emergence of a healing story marker is an excellent opportunity to help clients fully elaborate the fundamental importance of core attachment needs in their lives: to be loved and to matter. Healing stories can also serve as powerful exceptions to the negative expectations or rules that have come to define a client's same old story. They are not only restructuring a telling of the past but also, perhaps most important, opening the door for the anticipation of future possibilities and secure, trusting relationships with others. Her therapist identifies the emergence of a healing story marker when she skillfully helps Alex to disclose loving memories of childhood while Alex plays the role of her mother.

Therapist: Can you tell her some of those good qualities you want her to be comforted by, to be aware of? What are some things about her that she should be aware of?

Client: You remember, you remember my naturally curly hair and you used to sit there for hours? You and your sister insisted on doing my hair not one way, two ways, three ways. Do you know what? [Laughs] As an adult, that would take a lot of patience!

Therapist: [Laughs] So, "I had a lot of patience and I enjoyed you girls."

Client: I enjoyed you guys piling on top of me while we were watching TV, and we would all pile on top of one another. I really enjoyed the . . . think about helping me cooking: You'd be chopping, busy chopping and arguing with your sister or whatever. Remember the times when you were having temper tantrums and I was really comforting and calmed you down, when you'd go through utter destruction in your room and rip your room right apart. I remember the times that I never said very much to you; I let you do that. You would rip the mattress off and tear all the clothes out of your sister's cupboard. You would dump all of the shoes, the drawers, and everything all in the middle of the floor, only to have to come back an hour later and pick it all up anyways. [Laughs] So I'm not sure why you did that.

Therapist: So, it sounds like I kind of got a kick out of those parts of you.

Client: Yeah.

Therapist: Exasperating, but I kind of appreciated you; you need to know that.

Client: You, you had a real nick in you there. You always had a real answer for things; you were quite bright, and I had a hard time keeping up with you. You were very mischievous. Fortunately, you never harmed yourself, but your teasing, your lightheartedness, and your sense of humor . . .

Therapist: So, it sounds like you're saying I found you quite a delightful little girl.

Client: Those were good times, those were really good times.

Therapist: Hmm, those are beautiful memories.

Client: I would take you to the lake and going to my, to Grandma's house, helping Grandma with those donuts, and Grandma would be there baking, and you adored the pets, the animals that you had. That cat—God, I couldn't stand that cat, but you insisted on keeping that ratty old cat and the mice under your bed. That was [laughs], I don't know.

Therapist: Sounds like it warms your heart to think of those things.

Client: There were a lot of good times too. And it is difficult not to be negative and think of it in a negative way. It's . . .

Therapist: But it's important.

Client: It's very important.

Therapist: Can you come over here? [Client changes chairs.] So how are you feeling? Warm and . . .

Client: Yeah, I feel warm and I feel secure.

Therapist: Can you say that to her?

Client: It does make me feel more secure, loved. I liked feeling like that; it felt nice. Since you died, I have not been able to really feel that. I think I have to challenge everybody and everything. I feel like I have had to question people's motives. I feel [voice breaking] with my husband, with my siblings . . .

Significantly, it was only after Alex has been able to forgive her mother's decision to commit suicide when she was a 12-year-old child that these tender, healing memories of a loving engagement between mother and daughter are recalled and disclosed in her therapy sessions. As demonstrated in the foregoing example, the therapist's empathic responses play an important role in the client's sustained elaboration of her loving memories. In addition, the therapist's inquiry, "So how are you feeling?" in response to disclosing the memories helps the client to reflect on the importance of experiential feelings of warmth and trust that are evoked by her recollections.

In addition, the therapist's request to have the client tell her mother about these feelings enhances the sense of a loving bond and attachment connection between daughter and mother, a feeling that Alex had not experienced since her mother's sudden death many years ago. To help facilitate the development of a more integrative and compassionate view of herself in relation to her mother, the therapist might ask Alex, "And what does this mean to you, that you were loved by your mom as a little girl?" The capacity to be able to return to these recollections in the future, and to the imagined conversation with her mother, sets the stage for self-narrative reconstruction wherein Alex may begin to reintegrate a sense of having been loved by a mother who made a tragic mistake and asks for forgiveness.

As discussed in Chapter 4, narrative self-identity is reconstructed in three possible ways: by (a) the creation of a new self-narrative and new personal meanings by differentiating preexisting views of self or others, (b) the inception of a radical reorganization of the self-narrative and the articulation of new emotionally significant ways of viewing and understanding the self or others, and/or (c) the integration of disparate emotional experiences into a coherent self-narrative that produces a sense of relational security. It is important for Alex that the capacity to forgive her mother has enabled the articulation of past loving memories of their relationship (i.e., healing stories) that significantly affect her sense of emotional security, warmth, and trust in others.

CONCLUSION

Alex and her therapist undertook the important but difficult experiential work of disentangling and differentiating emotions and events of the suicide trauma such that a coherent narrative and emotion integration might be constructed. In particular, the narrative organization of painful emotions occurring before, during, and after her mother's suicide allowed the client to reflexively explore the emotional meaning of these experiences from new relational vantage points. Of particular importance was the emergence of the perspective of the loving mother, through empty-chair role-plays in the therapy sessions, and the coconstruction of a new account of her suicide story.

In addition, it appears that shifts to emotional differentiation and meaning making are key to the emergence of new, more satisfying and coherent ways of understanding clients' same old stories. The narrative organization of distressing emotional responses facilitates a reflexive processing of emotional memories, which can then be explored from different relational vantage points or perspectives. In turn, emotion shifts and new meanings emerge for clients while engaged in the movement from one relational vantage point to another. Greenberg (2002) argued that effective EFT therapists operate as emotion coaches for their clients. On the basis of the current analysis, it would appear that the therapist's shifts to both emotional differentiation and reflexive meaning making are essential for productive therapy.

Finally, the "mother's" validation of Alex's painful stories of terror, shame, sadness, and resentment enacted by Alex in the empty chair allowed Alex to empathically enter the imagined intrapersonal world of her mother's felt emotions, intentions, beliefs, and concerns at the time of her suicide. For the first time in her life, Alex constructs and accepts a coherent, compelling account of how a loving mother makes a terrible mistake and commits suicide. The emergence of a new understanding of the loving basis of her relationship with her mother results in the creation of an emotionally coherent, comprehensive, and integrative account of Alex's life story. In addition, through the disclosure of untold stories and healing memories, a more emotionally differentiated and coherent narrative of her relationship with her mother leads to the emergence of healing memories that evoke and instantiate lived experiences of being loved by her mother. The integration of these important attachment memories, and the warm sense of security and trust they evoke, is foundational to a new way of being with others in the world, a corrective emotional experience, and the basis for a new view of self.

8

CONCLUSION

With this book, we have attempted to outline why a combination of narrative and emotion is important for effective treatment practices in emotion-focused therapy (EFT). A main aspect of this synthesis is that meaning making without emotional grounding is unproductive and that emotion without narrative context remains undifferentiated and poorly understood. We also laid out an approach to help clients tolerate a wider range of emotional experiences—experiences that often went unacknowledged or were not understood—and to symbolize this experience in words to create meaning and a coherent narrative. When a client's awareness of self becomes more fully articulated and organized in narrative form, new understandings of self and others often emerge that lead to behavioral change and new ways of being in the world. In addition, the experience of accessing primary adaptive emotions leads to identity reconstruction and relational change, which help to sustain new, more satisfying ways of being in relation to others. When a new experience is symbolized in awareness and people reauthor their stories, the narrative change also leads to a sense of agency.

In a narrative-informed approach to EFT, emotionally meaningful stories are viewed as not only shaping clients' understanding of their personal worlds but also providing a foundation for the construction of a unique personal identity, new views of self and others, and a sense of security. By giving form and structure to even disconnected experiences and memories, narrative offers a space for self-reflection and self-construction that requires clients to interpret and make meaning of their most troubling and/or surprising life experiences. And it may well be that when clients are faced with a radically challenged sense of self and/or circumstance, they are impelled to become narrators as well as actors in their own life drama. As clients begin to author their own stories in therapy sessions, especially positive outcome stories that challenge negative expectations of the same old story, a unique opportunity arises to construct a more agentic and compassionate view of self and, possibly, a more meaningful and satisfying future life.

When clients face unexpected life challenges and losses, it may seem as if their lives are "out of phase" with the plots and themes of culturally shared story lines. It is precisely those personal experiences that challenge clients' existing views of self and are not easily accommodated by familiar cultural plotlines (McLeod, 2004; White, 2007) that are least likely to be disclosed to others as told stories. As a consequence, many of our clients' most important life experiences—as demonstrated in the case examples of Margaret and Alex—have remained unknown to others and "unstoried" for themselves, with little opportunity for meaningful reflection or integration into the corpus of autobiographical memory (ABM) narratives that "define" who they are.

Along with Bruner (2004), we believe that a sense of self originates in the embodied act of storying our lived experiences of the world. The integration of emotionally salient, lived stories is the foundation for personal identity and enables a sense of self-coherence and continuity over time. Once organized and externalized as a story, our subjective world of emotions, beliefs, and intentions can be shared with others, a storied "past" can be returned to for further self-understanding, and the hopes and dreams for an imagined future can be articulated. Self-identity over time is thus based on a narrative ordering. This identity is not real in the way that a "living body" is real. Rather, it is a unity that is constructed out of the many ways in which our lives and bodily felt experience can be narrated and described. What counts at any one point in time as "me" is therefore based on accessing events in my stream of experience that I most care about. The sense of identity, direction, agency, and a life plan are all grounded in the memorable connections of the stream.

A self-identity narrative emerges when body and past interact with present context and social and cultural norms. By unifying the events of an individual's life on the basis of *emplotment,* or narrative ordering, a sense of identity emerges that remains stable over time. More specifically, the narrative ordering of time and events provides unity and coherence to support the experience that one persists as a unique self. ABMs organized according to self-defining themes provide us with a sense of who we were and who we are and give us a sense of purpose, unity, and identity. Long-term memory thus offers a rich, thick sense of personal identity: knowing who one is and where one comes from.

EMOTION AND NARRATIVE PROCESS

As we have argued in this book, a narrative-informed EFT approach takes emotion as the fundamental datum of human experience while recognizing the importance of narrative contextualization for new meaning making. Emotion and cognition are viewed as inextricably linked through story (Greenberg, 2002; Greenberg & Angus, 2004) in this model. Drawing from a broad range of researchers and clinicians, we view emotions as centrally important in the experience of self, in both adaptive and maladaptive functioning, and for therapeutic change. Optimal adaptation, however, is seen as involving a narrative synthesis of affect and cognition for personal identity reconstruction and the development of a secure sense of self. A major premise guiding intervention in narrative-informed EFT is that if you do not accept yourself as you are, you cannot make yourself available for transformation. Because clients need to fully experience their feelings in order to change them, therapists help clients arrive at their core emotional experience by becoming aware of it and symbolizing it in a narrative context. This enhances emotion regulation, acceptance, and reflection. First, clients need to experience the maladaptive emotions that have shaped the plotlines of their same old stories, such as fear of being abandoned by a loved one or anger at feeling violated by an alcoholic father. Next, the therapist helps them transform their same old stories by facilitating the generation of alternate emotional responses that generate new plotlines, such as grief at the loss of a loved one or compassion for one's father's troubled childhood, that in turn facilitate the construction of new narratives based on these feelings.

In addition, we have argued that emotion and narrative are integrated at the level of tacit emotion schemes, which are structured in a narrative form with an unfolding sequence of actions being taken and consequences that occur. Thus, scheme activation is not a simple associationistic process, nor is a scheme simply a structure, but it functions as an unfolding of a process representing that this happened in this sequence in this context with this implication. These emotion schemes then generate the lived story of our lives.

In narrative-informed EFT, tacit experiences associated with the evoked affective reaction are made explicit and put into narrative form. In essence, a synthesis occurs between the tacit representation of felt emotional experiences, the imaginal representation of the wordless narrative scene, and verbal symbolization (Damasio, 1999). The narrative scaffolding of emotional experiences provides an effective framework for the organization and integration of felt emotions, unfolding action sequences, and the told story of our lives. It is clear that in therapy, stories emerge from the body when there is a facilitative listener present to receive them; they are brought into "being" through language.

The told story of our lives is a higher level construction based on further processing of emotion, but it is equally fundamental to human nature. Out of the evolutionary need to maintain the coherence of the organism against threats to its physical integrity grew a self that needs to maintain its coherence at a level of psychological identity and that needs to master the environment to survive. As our basic survival needs became more assured, and conceptual and language abilities more developed, our capacity to sustain a stable, coherent sense of self and others became as important for survival as our sense of physical health and well-being. Damage to the self's identity or disruption of its coherence was experienced as a threat to survival. Then, maintaining a coherent narrative identity became as important as maintaining physical coherence.

The concept of the narrative self, however, implies a hierarchy of defining features of humanity where linguistic ability is at the top and abilities of an emotional and somatic kind are inevitably lower down in the processing hierarchy. This, however, does not mean they are of lesser importance. Inarticulate emotional and bodily features of human beings are crucial aspects of human experience and must therefore be included in any adequate theory of identity. Although identity in large part is linguistically created, sustained, and informed, not all self-interpretation needs verbalization. We also possess an evolving nonlinguistic sense of who we are, of what is important to oneself, and of how one wants to live one's life. A person's cares, concerns, and projects are revealed in how the person lives. This is the lived story with which the told story may or may not cohere. An important goal of therapy is to bring the lived story and the told story into harmony.

There also needs to be a constant interplay of an embodied and emotional subject in a life–world where constellations of identity are formed and reformed. It is the embodied and temporal nature of the narrative self that prevents it from being seen as a substance on the one hand or as a purely social construction on the other. Given that corporeality is basic to the human condition, then the possibility of the self being simply a social construction is incoherent. The very nature of human embodiment means that different dimensions of human identity (e.g., being female, visually impaired, feeling exhausted) cannot be instantly transformed by a simple act of narrative construction. Corporeality lends stability to the narrative self, but how we make sense of and story our corporeality codetermines their significance.

THEORY OF PRACTICE

In this book we have also offered a narrative-informed approach to the practice of EFT. Clients come to therapy because they no longer know how to tell a story of their lives that works for them, and the meaning they are making of emotionally salient experiences—to form coherent narratives—has ceased to function smoothly or perhaps has never functioned well at all. Thus, rather than seeing the client as independently discovering new personal meanings, in a narrative-informed approach to EFT we believe that both therapists and client contribute to the coconstruction of new personal meanings and narrative reconstruction. Therapy is conducted mainly thorough the expression of words and the shared elaboration of the client's self, allowing clients to feel more secure and experience deeply the emotional intensity, and hence meaningfulness, of their own lives. Therapists thus need to work with clients to coconstruct a narrative framework that works, using the right words fused with the right feelings at the right time. Therapists play an essential role in helping clients to disclose their most vulnerable stories for further emotional differentiation and new meaning making, and it is the therapist's capacity to empathically attune to clients' emerging emotional experiences that provides a safe and trusting space for clients to access, disclose, and reexperience often painful autobiographical emotional memories. In addition, therapists help clients organize their painful emotions for further reflection by actively identifying specific situational contexts and cues that help contain and explain emotional experiences.

A defining feature of the narrative-informed EFT approach is that intervention is marker guided, so in addition to the empathic, narrative explication of experience, therapists also engage in marker-guided interventions. Narrative-informed EFT therefore builds on an empathic relational approach by identifying a variety of context-specific forms of intervention that depend on the in-session situation and client state. In this volume we have identified a set of narrative markers to further inform the practice of EFT and to alert narratively oriented therapists of other orientations to important opportunities for effectively working with emotions, using specific interventions. The marker-guided form of intervention we have suggested promotes different levels of change by transforming lived experience into self-narrative reconstruction in different ways at different markers.

Intensive analysis of therapy tapes has found that clients enter specific narrative-emotion states that are identifiable by in-session statements and behaviors that mark underlying narrative-emotion types of processing that afford opportunities for particular types of effective intervention. Clients' narrative-emotion markers indicate not only the type of intervention to use but also clients' current readiness to work on these problems. Narrative-informed EFT thus involves the identification of markers of different types of narrative-emotion processing states and specific ways of intervening that best suit these problems.

Each of the markers has been studied and specified, and some of the key aspects of intervention at each marker have begun to be specified. Although all interventions share a common empathic base, they differ in the degree to which specific ABMs are evoked, the degree of context elaboration needed, the degree of symbolization of bodily felt experience and emotion, the degree of promoting story coherence, and the degree of noticing and heightening client experiences. The problem markers that were identified were same old story (i.e., repetitive unproductive experience based on core maladaptive emotion schemes), unstoried emotions (i.e., states of undifferentiated affect and disregulated emotional states), empty stories (i.e., clients' ABM disclosures that are stripped of lived emotional experience), and broken stories (i.e., experiences of self-narrative and emotion incoherence).

In addition, an important innovation that emerged from the narrative-informed study of transcripts was the identification of emergent meaning markers that highlight opportunities for therapists to recognize and enhance change that the client reports has already occurred, rather than only focusing intervention on problems yet to be resolved. The three emergent meaning markers identified were untold stories, unique outcome stories, and healing stories. Each of these narrative-emotion markers was shown to provide therapists with an opportunity to use specific interventions to help their clients more fully elaborate their most important personal stories. Untold stories are those that occur in therapy when the therapist hears the client speak about emotionally salient personal experiences that have not yet been externalized as told stories. Unique outcome stories occur at times when clients express surprise, excitement, contentment, or inner peace when comparing present adaptive experience with past maladaptive experience. Finally, healing outcome stories are those that occur when clients convey an unexpected recollection of a vivid personal memory in which an important relational need was met by a significant other. Features of optimal therapist interventions for all the markers were discussed, and the end states achieved by the different processes at each point were described.

IMPLICATIONS FOR FUTURE TREATMENT PROGRAMS AND RESEARCH

Opportunities for the study of further narrative-emotion change processes abound, and methods of process and task analysis and qualitative and quantitative methods and measures have been developed to enable these kinds of studies (Angus, Lewin, Bouffard, & Rotondi-Trevisan, 2004; Greenberg, 2007). Already, a number of narrative-emotion tasks have been defined (Bryntwick, 2009) and evaluated in both good and poor outcome EFT treatments, and the promising research findings merit further study. In particular, it will be important to identify the specific steps and strategies used by effective EFT therapists to help clients shift from unproductive engagement in same old stories to accessing and symbolizing primary emotions for adaptive action tendencies and new story outcomes. New tasks also need to be described by explicating clinicians' implicit knowledge of the process of in-session change.

A crucial next step is having narrative-emotion training introduced into graduate programs and for practicing clinicians. Training students and clinicians in the importance of identifying micro- and macronarratives and of narrative restructuring, and providing specific training in marker identification and intervention, will enhance their sensitivity to the narrative aspects of treatment. First, the generic relational narrative-emotion approach could benefit all trainees, and this would be enhanced by training in the specific marker-guided intervention approach. In training programs committed to teaching evidence-based treatments that have emphasized cognitive behavior therapy to the exclusion of other approaches, the evidence is now strong enough for us to recommend that EFT should be required as part of a training program and offered as an important addition to more symptom-focused coping-skills approaches. Students' education as psychologists is incomplete without a greater emphasis on training in skills of working with narrative-emotion attunement.

CONCLUSION

In EFT, we have moved from a client-centered, core-conditions model (Rogers, 1957) to a more interpersonal, coconstructive (Angus et al., 2004) therapeutic style that integrates being with the client (i.e., being full present and bringing specific relationship qualities to bear) and doing things with the client (i.e., guiding the client by intervening in different ways at different times) for effective therapeutic outcomes. Following and guiding are now seen as a kind of synergistic dance that shapes therapists' engagement with clients during the therapy hour. We view therapist relationship qualities such as empathic attunement, prizing, genuineness, acceptance, and validation of the client's experience as contributing to the creation of a secure, relational bond and an overall productive working alliance. It is when clients feel safe and truly heard by their therapist that they can fully access and disclose their most vulnerable and painful lived stories for further emotional differentiation, transformation, restorying, and new meaning making. Markers of different narrative-emotion states that are amenable to differential intervention then arise in this type of relational context. Thus, rather than seeing the client as independently discovering new personal meanings, in a narrative-informed approach to EFT we believe that in productive EFT sessions both therapists and clients contribute to the coconstruction of new personal meanings and narrative reconstruction. In addition, we see therapists as offering expertise in guiding deeper exploration and meaning making and promoting integration of emotion and reflection to help clients restory experience.

REFERENCES

Adams, K. (2010). *Therapist influence on depressed clients' therapeutic experiencing and outcome* (Unpublished doctoral dissertation). York University, Toronto, Canada.

Ainsworth, M. D. (1979). Infant–mother attachment. *American Psychologist, 34,* 932–937. doi:10.1037/0003-066X.34.10.932

Ainsworth, M. D. (1989). Attachments beyond infancy. *American Psychologist, 44,* 709–716. doi:10.1037/0003-066X.44.4.709

American Psychological Association. (Producer). (2007). *Series 1: Systems of Psychotherapy. Narrative Therapy* [DVD]. Available from http://www.apa.org/videos/

Angus, L., & Bouffard, B. (2004). The search for emotional meaning and self-coherence in the face of traumatic loss in childhood: A narrative process perspective. In J. D. Raskin & S. K. Bridges (Eds.), *Studies in meaning: Bridging the personal and social in constructivist Psychology* (Vol. 2, pp. 312–322). New York, NY: Pace University Press.

Angus, L. & Bouffard-Bowes, B. (2002). No lo entiendo: La busqueda de sentido emocional y coherencia personalante una perdida traumatica durante la infancia [I just do not understand: The search for emotional coherence after traumatic loss in childhood]. *Revista Psicoterapia, XII*(49), 25–46.

Angus, L., & Hardtke, K. (1994). Narrative processes in psychotherapy. *Canadian Psychology, 35,* 190–203. doi:10.1037/0708-5591.35.2.190

Angus, L., & Hardtke, K. (2007). Insight and story change in brief experiential therapy for depression: An intensive narrative process analysis. In L. Castonguay & C. Hill (Eds.), *Insight in psychotherapy* (pp. 187–207). Washington, DC: American Psychological Association.

Angus, L., Hardtke, K., & Levitt, H. (1996). *Narrative processes coding system: Coding assistance manual.* Toronto, Canada: York University Narrative Research Lab.

Angus, L., & Kagan, F. (2007). Empathic relational bonds and personal agency in psychotherapy: Implications for psychotherapy supervision, practice, and research. *Psychotherapy: Theory/Research/Practice/Training, 44,* 371–377.

Angus, L. E., & Kagan, F. (2009). Therapist empathy and client anxiety reduction in motivational interviewing: "She carries with me, the experience." *Journal of Clinical Psychology, 65,* 1156–1167. doi:10.1002/jclp.20635

Angus, L., & Korman, Y. (2002). Coherence, conflict, and change in brief therapy: A metaphor theme analysis. In S. Fussell (Ed.), *The verbal communication of emotions: Interdisciplinary perspectives* (pp. 151–165). Mahwah, NJ: Erlbaum.

Angus, L., Levitt, H., & Hardtke, K. (1999). The Narrative Processes Coding System: Research applications and implications for psychotherapy practice. *Journal of Clinical Psychology, 55,* 1255–1270. doi:10.1002/(SICI)1097-4679(199910)55:10<1255::AID-JCLP7>3.0.CO;2-F

Angus, L., Lewin, J., Bouffard, B., & Rotondi-Trevisan, D. (2004). "What's the story?" Working with narrative in experiential psychotherapy. In L. Angus & J. McLeod (Eds.), *Handbook of narrative and psychotherapy: Practice, theory, and research* (pp. 87–101). Thousand Oaks, CA: Sage.

Angus, L., & Macaulay, H. (2010). *Expressed empathy*. Retrieved from http://www.commonlanguagepsychotherapy.org/fileadmin/user_upload/Accepted_procedures/expressedempathy.pdf

Angus, L., & McLeod, J. (Eds.). (2004a). *The handbook of narrative and psychotherapy: Practice, theory, and research.* Thousand Oaks, CA: Sage.

Angus, L., & McLeod, J. (2004b). Self-multiplicity and narrative expression in psychotherapy. In H. J. M. Hermans & G. Dimaggio (Eds.), *The dialogical self in psychotherapy* (pp. 77–90). New York, NY: Brunner-Routledge. doi:10.4324/9780203314616_chapter_5

Angus, L., & Rennie, D. (1988). Therapist participation in metaphor generation: Collaborative and noncollaborative styles. *Psychotherapy: Theory, Research, & Practice, 25*, 552–560.

Angus, L., & Rennie, D. (1989). Envisioning the representational world: Metaphoric expression in psychotherapy relationships. *Psychotherapy: Theory, Research, & Practice, 26*, 372–379.

Arciero, G., & Guidano, V. (2000). Experience, explanation, and the quest for coherence. In R. Neimeyer & J. Raskin (Eds.), *Constructions of disorder: Meaning-making frameworks for psychotherapy* (pp. 1–118). Washington, DC: American Psychological Association.

Bandura, A. (2006). Toward a psychology of human agency. *Perspectives on Psychological Science, 1*, 164–180. doi:10.1111/j.1745-6916.2006.00011.x

Barrett-Lennard, G. T. (1986). The Relationship Inventory now: Issues and advances in theory, method, and use. In L. S. Greenberg & W. M. Pinsof (Eds.), *The psychotherapeutic process: A research handbook* (pp. 439–476). New York, NY: Guilford Press.

Bartholomew, K., & Horowitz, L. M. (1991). Attachment styles among young adults: A test of a four-category model. *Journal of Personality and Social Psychology, 61*, 226–244. doi:10.1037/0022-3514.61.2.226

Baumeister, R. F., & Newman, L. S. (1994). How stories make sense of personal experiences: Motives that shape autobiographical narratives. *Personality and Social Psychology Bulletin, 20*, 676–690. doi:10.1177/0146167294206006

Beck, A. (1976). *Cognitive therapies and the emotional disorders.* New York, NY: International Universities Press.

Bordin, E. S. (1979). The generalizability of the psychoanalytic concept of the working alliance. *Psychotherapy: Theory, Research, & Practice, 16*, 252–260. doi:10.1037/h0085885

Boritz, T., Angus, L., Monette, G., & Hollis-Walker, L. (2008). An empirical analysis of autobiographical memory specificity subtypes in brief emotion-focused and client-centered treatments of depression. *Psychotherapy Research, 18*, 584–593.

Boritz, T., Angus, L., Monette, G., & Hollis-Walker, L. (2011). Narrative and emotion integration in psychotherapy: Investigating the relationship between autobiographical memory specificity and expressed emotional arousal in brief emotion-focused and client-centered treatments of depression. *Psychotherapy Research, 21,* 16–26.

Borkovec, T., Roemer, L., & Kinyon, J. (1995). Disclosure and worry: Opposite sides of the emotional processing coin. In J. W. Pennebaker (Ed.), *Emotion, disclosure, & health* (pp. 47–70). Washington, DC: American Psychological Association. doi:10.1037/10182-003

Bowlby, J. (1969). *Attachment and loss: Vol. 1. Attachment.* New York, NY: Basic Books.

Bowlby, J. (1988). *A secure base.* New York, NY: Basic Books.

Bruner, J. S. (1986). *Actual minds, possible worlds.* Cambridge, MA: Harvard University Press.

Bruner, J. (2002). *Making stories: Law, literature, life.* New York, NY: Farrar, Straus & Giroux.

Bruner, J. S. (2004). The narrative creation of self. In L. Angus & J. McLeod (Eds.), *Handbook of narrative and psychotherapy: Practice, theory, and research* (pp. 15–29). Thousand Oaks, CA: Sage.

Bryntwick, E. (2009). *The development and application of the narrative-emotion integration coding system in brief emotion-focused and client-centred treatment of depression* (Unpublished master's thesis). York University, Toronto, Canada.

Bryntwick, E., Angus, L., Boritz, T., & Greenberg, L. (2011). *The development and application of the narrative-emotion integration coding system in brief emotion-focused and client-centred treatment of depression.* Manuscript submitted for publication.

Bucci, W. (1995). The power of the narrative: A multiple code account. In J. W. Pennebaker (Ed.), *Emotion, disclosure, & health* (pp. 93–124). Washington, DC: American Psychological Association. doi:10.1037/10182-005

Carryer, J., & Greenberg, L. (2010). Optimal levels of emotional arousal in experiential therapy of depression. *Journal of Consulting and Clinical Psychology, 78,* 190–199.

Castonguay, L. G. (2005). Training issues in psychotherapy integration: A commentary. *Journal of Psychotherapy Integration, 15,* 384–391. doi:10.1037/1053-0479.15.4.384

Castonguay, L. G., & Beutler, L. E. (Eds.). (2006). *Principles of therapeutic change that work.* New York, NY: Oxford University Press.

Castonguay, L. G., & Hill, C. (Eds.). (2007). *Insight in psychotherapy.* Washington, DC: American Psychological Association. doi:10.1037/11532-000

Combs, G., & Freedman, J. (2004). A poststructuralist approach to narrative work. In L. Angus & J. McLeod (Eds.), *Handbook of narrative and psychotherapy: Practice, theory, and research* (pp. 137–155). Thousand Oaks, CA: Sage.

Conway, M. A., & Pleydell-Pearce, C. W. (2000). The construction of autobiographical memories in the self-memory system. *Psychological Review, 107,* 261–288. doi:10.1037/0033-295X.107.2.261

Damasio, A. (1999). *The feeling of what happens.* New York, NY: Harcourt Brace.

Derogatis, L. R., Rickels, K., & Roch, A. F. (1976). The SCL-90 and the MMPI: A step in the validation of a new self-report scale. *The British Journal of Psychiatry, 128,* 280–289. doi:10.1192/bjp.128.3.280

de Saint-Exupéry, A. (1943). *The little prince.* New York, NY: Harcourt, Brace.

Dimaggio, G., & Semeraris, A. (2004). Disorganized narratives: The psychological condition and its treatment. In L. Angus & J. McLeod (Eds.), *Handbook of narrative and psychotherapy: Practice, theory, and research* (pp. 263–283). Thousand Oaks, CA: Sage.

Elliott, R., Greenberg, L., & Lietaer, G. (2004). Research on experiential psychotherapy. In M. Lambert (Ed.), *Bergin and Garfield's handbook of psychotherapy and behavior change* (pp. 493–539). New York, NY: Wiley.

Ellison, J. A., Greenberg, L., Goldman, R., & Angus, L. (2009). Maintenance of gains at follow-up in experiential therapies for depression. *Journal of Consulting and Clinical Psychology, 77,* 103–112. doi:10.1037/a0014653

Elliott, R., Watson, J. C., Goldman, R. N., & Greenberg, L. S. (2004). *Learning emotion-focused therapy: The process-experiential approach to change.* Washington, DC: American Psychological Association.

Epstein, S. (1984). Controversial issues in emotion theory. In P. Shaver (Ed.), *Review of personality and social psychology: Emotions, relationships and health* (pp. 64–87). Beverly Hills, CA: Sage.

Frank, J. D. (1961). *Persuasion and healing.* Baltimore, MD: Johns Hopkins University Press.

Gendlin, E. T. (1996). *Focusing-oriented psychotherapy: A manual of the experiential method.* New York, NY: Guilford Press.

Goldfried, M. R. (2003). Cognitive–behavior therapy: Reflections on the evolution of a therapeutic orientation. *Cognitive Therapy and Research, 27,* 53–69. doi:10.1023/A:1022586629843

Goldman, R., Greenberg, L., & Angus, L. (2006). The effects of specific emotion-focused interventions and the therapeutic relationship in the treatment of depression: A dismantling study. *Psychotherapy Research, 16,* 527–549.

Goldman, R., Greenberg, L. S., & Pos, A. E. (2005). Depth of emotional experience and outcome. *Psychotherapy Research, 15,* 248–260. doi:10.1080/10503300512331385188

Gonçalves, O., Henriques, M., & Machado, P. (2004). Nurturing nature: Cognitive narrative strategies. In L. Angus & J. McLeod (Eds.), *Handbook of narrative and psychotherapy: Practice, theory, and research* (pp. 103–117). Thousand Oaks, CA: Sage.

Gonçalves, M., Mendes, I., Ribeiro, A., Angus, L., & Greenberg, L. (2010). Innovative moments and change in emotion-focused therapy: The case of Lisa. *Journal of Constructivist Psychology, 23,* 267–294.

Greenberg, L. S. (2002). *Emotion-focused therapy: Coaching clients to work through their feelings*. Washington, DC: American Psychological Association. doi:10.1037/10447-000

Greenberg, L. (2007). A guide to conducting a task analysis of psychotherapeutic change. *Psychotherapy Research, 17,* 15–30. doi:10.1080/10503300600720390

Greenberg, L. (2010). *Emotion-focused therapy*. Washington, DC: American Psychological Association.

Greenberg, L., & Angus, L. (2004). The contributions of emotion processes to narrative change in psychotherapy: A dialectical constructivist approach. In L. Angus & J. McLeod (Eds.), *Handbook of narrative psychotherapy: Practice, theory, and research* (pp. 331–349). Thousand Oaks, CA: Sage.

Greenberg, L. S., Auszra, L., & Herrmann, I. R. (2007). The relationship among emotional productivity, emotional arousal, and outcome in experiential therapy of depression. *Psychotherapy Research, 17,* 482–493. doi:10.1080/10503300600977800

Greenberg, L. S., Elliott, R. K., & Lietaer, G. (1994). Research on experiential psychotherapist. In A. E. Bergin & S. L. Garfield (Eds.), *Handbook of psychotherapy and behavior change* (4th ed., pp. 509–539). Oxford, England: Wiley.

Greenberg, L. S., Ford, C. L., Alden, L. S., & Johnson, S. M. (1993). In-session change in emotionally focused therapy. *Journal of Consulting and Clinical Psychology, 61,* 78–84. doi:10.1037/0022-006X.61.1.78

Greenberg, L., & Goldman, R. (2007). Case formulation in emotion-focused therapy. In T. Ells (Ed.), *Handbook of psychotherapy case formulation* (pp. 379–412). New York, NY: Guilford Press.

Greenberg, L. S., & Goldman, R. N. (2008). *Emotion-focused couples therapy: The dynamics of emotion, love, and power*. Washington, DC: American Psychological Association. doi:10.1037/11750-000

Greenberg, L. S., & Korman, L. (1993). Assimilating emotion into psychotherapy integration. *Journal of Psychotherapy Integration, 3,* 249–265.

Greenberg, L. S., & Malcolm, W. (2002). Resolving unfinished business: Relating process to outcome. *Journal of Consulting and Clinical Psychology, 70,* 406–416. doi:10.1037/0022-006X.70.2.406

Greenberg, L. S., & Paivio, S. C. (1997). *Working with emotions in psychotherapy*. New York, NY: Guilford Press.

Greenberg, L. S., & Pascual-Leone, J. (1995). A dialectical constructivist approach to experiential change. In R. A. Neimeyer & M. J. Mahoney (Eds.), *Constructivism in psychotherapy* (pp. 169–191). Washington, DC: American Psychological Association. doi:10.1037/10170-008

Greenberg, L. S., & Pascual-Leone, J. (1997). Emotion in the creation of personal meaning. In M. J. Power & C. R. Brewin (Eds.), *The transformation of meaning in psychological therapies: Integrating theory and practice* (pp. 157–173). Hoboken, NJ: Wiley.

Greenberg, L., & Pascual-Leone, J. (2001). J. A dialectical constructivist view of the creation of personal meaning. *Journal of Constructivist Psychology, 14,* 165–186. doi:10.1080/10720530151143539

Greenberg, L., Rice, L., & Elliott, R. (1993). *Facilitating emotional change.* New York, NY: Guilford Press.

Greenberg, L. S., & Safran, J. D. (1987). *Emotion in psychotherapy: Affect, cognition, and the process of change.* New York, NY: Guilford Press.

Greenberg, L. S., & Van Balen, R. (1998). The theory of experience-centered therapies. In L. S. Greenberg, J. C. Watson, & G. Lietaer (Eds.), *Handbook of experiential psychotherapy* (pp. 28–57). New York, NY: Guilford Press.

Greenberg, L. S., Warwar, S. H., & Malcolm, W. M. (2008). Differential effects of emotion-focused therapy and psychoeducation in facilitating forgiveness and letting go of emotional injuries. *Journal of Counseling Psychology, 55,* 185–196. doi:10.1037/0022-0167.55.2.185

Greenberg, L., & Watson, J. (1998). Experiential therapy of depression: Differential effects of client-centered relationship conditions and process experiential interventions. *Psychotherapy Research, 8,* 210–224.

Greenberg, L. S., & Watson, J. C. (2006). *Emotion-focused therapy for depression.* Washington, DC: American Psychological Association. doi:10.1037/11286-000

Greenberg, L. S., Watson, J. C., & Goldman, R. (1998). Process-experiential therapy for depression. In L. S. Greenberg, J. C. Watson, & R. Goldman (Eds.), *Handbook of experiential psychotherapy* (pp. 227–248). New York, NY: Guilford Press.

Gross, J. J. (2002). Emotion regulation: Affective, cognitive, and social consequences. *Psychophysiology, 39,* 281–291. doi:10.1017/S0048577201393198

Guidano, V. F. (1991). *The self in process.* New York, NY: Guilford Press.

Guidano, V. F. (1995). Self-observation in constructivist therapy. In R. A. Neimeyer & M. J. Mahoney (Eds.), *Constructivism in psychotherapy* (pp. 155–168). Washington, DC: American Psychological Association. doi:10.1037/10170-007

Habermas, T., & Bluck, S. (2000). Getting a life: The emergence of the life story in adolescence. *Psychological Bulletin, 126,* 748–769. doi:10.1037/0033-2909.126.5.748

Harber, K. D., & Pennebaker, J. W. (1992). Overcoming traumatic memories. In S. Christianson (Ed.), *The handbook of emotion and memory: Research and theory* (pp. 359–387). Hillsdale, NY: Erlbaum.

Hardtke, K., & Angus, L. (2004). The narrative assessment interview: Assessing self-change in psychotherapy. In L. Angus & J. McLeod (Eds.), *Handbook of narrative and psychotherapy: Practice, theory, and research* (pp. 247–262). Thousand Oaks, CA: Sage.

Harlow, H. (1958). The nature of love. *American Psychologist, 13,* 673–685. doi:10.1037/h0047884

Horvath, A. O., & Greenberg, L. S. (1989). Development and validation of the Working Alliance Inventory. *Journal of Counseling Psychology, 36,* 223–233. doi:10.1037/0022-0167.36.2.223

Howard, G. S. (1991). Culture tales: A narrative approach to thinking, cross-culture psychology, and psychotherapy. *American Psychologist, 46,* 187–197. doi:10.1037/0003-066X.46.3.187

Kagan, F., & Angus, L. (2010). *A whole new me: Identity construction and self-narrative change in psychotherapy.* Manuscript submitted for publication.

Lewin, J. K. (2001). *Both sides of the coin: Comparative analyses of narrative process patterns in poor and good outcome dyads engaged in brief experiential psychotherapy for depression* (Unpublished master's thesis). York University, Toronto, Ontario, Canada.

Lieberman, M., Eisenberg, M., Crockett, T., Tom, S., Pfeifer, J., & Baldwin, M. (2004). Putting feelings into words: Affect labeling disrupts amygdala activity in response to affective stimuli. *Psychological Science, 18,* 421–428.

Linehan, M. M. (1993). *Cognitive–behavioral treatment of borderline personality disorder.* New York, NY: Guilford Press.

Luborsky, L., & Crits-Christoph, P. (1990). *Understanding transference: The CCRT method.* New York, NY: Basic Books.

Mahoney, M. (1991). *Human change processes.* New York, NY: Basic Books.

Mallinckrodt, B. (1991). Client's representations of childhood emotional bonds with parents, social support, and formation of the working alliance. *Journal of Counseling Psychology, 38,* 401–409. doi:10.1037/0022-0167.38.4.401

McAdams, D., & Janis, L. (2004). Narrative identity and narrative therapy. In L. Angus & J. McLeod, *Handbook of narrative psychotherapy: Practice, theory, and research* (pp. 159–174). Thousand Oaks, CA: Sage.

McGaugh, J. L. (2000, January 14). Memory: A century of consolidation. *Science, 287,* 248–251. doi:10.1126/science.287.5451.248

McLeod, J. (2004). Social constructionism, narrative, and psychotherapy. In L. Angus & J. McLeod (Eds.), *Handbook of narrative and psychotherapy: Practice, theory, and research* (pp. 351–365). Thousand Oaks, CA: Sage.

McLeod, J., & Balamoutsou, S. (2000). Narrative process in the assimilation of a problematic experience: Qualitative analysis of a single case. *Zeitschrift fur qualitative bildungs, 2,* 283–302.

Mendes, I., Ribeiro, A., Angus, L., Greenberg, L., Sousa, I., & Gonçalves, M. (2010). Narrative change in emotion-focused therapy: How is change constructed through the lens of the innovative moments coding system? *Psychotherapy Research, 20,* 692–701. doi:10.1080/10503307.2010.514960

Missirlian, T. M., Toukmanian, S. G., Warwar, S. H., & Greenberg, L. S. (2005). Emotional arousal, client perceptual processing, and the working alliance in experiential psychotherapy for depression. *Journal of Consulting and Clinical Psychology, 73,* 861–871. doi:10.1037/0022-006X.73.5.861

Nadel, L., & Moscovitch, M. (1997). Memory consolidation, retrograde amnesia, and the hippocampal complex. *Current Opinion in Neurobiology, 7,* 217–227.

Neimeyer, R. (1995). Client-generated narratives in psychotherapy. In R. Neimeyer & M. Mahoney (Eds.), *Constructivism in psychotherapy* (pp. 231–246). Washington, DC: American Psychological Association. doi:10.1037/10170-010

Nelson, K. (1989). *Narratives from the crib.* Cambridge, MA: Harvard University Press.

Nelson, K., & Fivush, R. (2004). Emergence of autobiographical memory. *Psychological Review, 111,* 486–511. doi:10.1037/0033-295X.111.2.486

Orlinsky, D. E., Grawe, K., & Parks, B. K. (1994). Process and outcome in psychotherapy. In A. E. Bergin & S. L. Garfield (Eds.), *Handbook of psychotherapy and behavior change* (4th ed., pp. 270–376). New York, NY: Wiley.

Pachankis, J., & Goldfried, M. R. (2007). An integrative principle-based approach to psychotherapy integration. In G. Hofman & J. Weinberger (Eds.), *The art and science of psychotherapy* (pp. 49–68). New York, NY: Brunner-Routledge.

Paivio, S. C., & Greenberg, L. S. (1995). Resolving "unfinished business": Efficacy of experiential therapy using empty-chair dialogue. *Journal of Consulting and Clinical Psychology, 63,* 419–425. doi:10.1037/0022-006X.63.3.419

Paivio, S. C., & Pascual-Leone, A. (2010). *Emotion-focused therapy for complex trauma: An integrative approach.* Washington, DC: American Psychological Association. doi:10.1037/12077-002

Pascual-Leone, A., & Greenberg, L. (2007). Emotional Processing in Experiential Therapy: Why "the only way out is through." *Journal of Consulting and Clinical Psychology, 75,* 875–887. doi:10.1037/0022-006X.75.6.875

Pascual-Leone, J. (1987). Organismic processes for neo-Piagetian theories: A dialectical causal account of cognitive development. *International Journal of Psychology, 22,* 531–570. doi:10.1080/00207598708246795

Pascual-Leone, J. (1990a). An essay on wisdom: Toward organismic processes that make it possible. In R. J. Sternberg (Ed.), *Wisdom: Its nature, origins, and development* (pp. 244–278). New York, NY: Cambridge University Press.

Pascual-Leone, J. (1990b). Reflections on life-span intelligence, consciousness, and ego development. In C. Alexander & E. Langer (Eds.), *Higher stages of human development: Perspectives on adult growth* (pp. 258–285). New York, NY: Oxford University Press.

Pascual-Leone, J. (1991). Emotions, development and psychotherapy: A dialectical constructivist perspective. In J. Safran & L. Greenberg (Eds.), *Emotion, psychotherapy, and change* (pp. 302–335). New York, NY: Guilford Press.

Pellowski, A. (1977). *The world of storytelling.* New York, NY: Bowker.

Pennebaker, J. W. (1995). *Emotion, disclosure, & health.* Washington, DC: American Psychological Association. doi:10.1037/10182-000

Pennebaker, J. W., & Seagal, J. (1999). Forming a story: The health benefits of narrative. *Journal of Clinical Psychology, 55,* 1243–1254. doi:10.1002/(SICI)1097-4679(199910)55:10<1243::AID-JCLP6>3.0.CO;2-N

Perls, F., Hefferline, R. F., & Goodman, P. (1951). *Gestalt therapy*. New York, NY: Dell.

Polkinghorne, D. (2004). Narrative therapy and postmodernism. In L. Angus & J. McLeod (Eds.), *Handbook of narrative and psychotherapy: Practice, theory, and research* (pp. 53–68). Thousand Oaks, CA: Sage.

Pos, A. E., Greenberg, L. S., Goldman, R. N., & Korman, L. M. (2003). Emotional processing during experiential treatment of depression. *Journal of Consulting and Clinical Psychology, 71*, 1007–1016. doi:10.1037/0022-006X.71.6.1007

Rice, L., & Greenberg, L. (Eds.). (1984). *Patterns of change: An intensive analysis of psychotherapeutic process*. New York, NY: Guilford Press.

Rogers, C. R. (1951). *Client-centered therapy*. New York, NY: Houghton Mifflin.

Rogers, C. R. (1957). The necessary and sufficient conditions of therapeutic personality change. *Journal of Consulting Psychology, 21*, 95. doi:10.1037/h0045357

Rogers, C. R. (1959). A theory of therapy, personality, and interpersonal relationships, as developed in the client-centered framework. In S. Koch (Ed.), *Psychology: A study of a science* (pp. 184–256). New York, NY: McGraw-Hill.

Rogers, C. R. (1975). Empathy: An unappreciated way of being. *The Counseling Psychologist, 5*(2), 2–10. doi:10.1177/001100007500500202

Rushdie, S. (1992). One thousand days in a balloon. In S. Rushdie (Ed.), *Imaginary homelands: Essays and criticism, 1981–1991* (pp. 430–439). London, England: Granta.

Safran, J. D., & Muran, J. C. (2000). *Negotiating the therapeutic alliance*. New York, NY: Guilford Press.

Sarbin, T. (1986). *Narrative psychology: The storied nature of human conduct*. New York, NY: Praeger.

Singer, J., & Blagov, P. (2004). Self-defining memories, narrative identity, and psychotherapy: A conceptual model, empirical investigation, and case report. In L. Angus & J. McLeod (Eds.), *Handbook of narrative and psychotherapy: Practice, theory, and research*. Thousand Oaks, CA: Sage.

Singer, J., & Salovey, P. (1993). *The remembered self: Emotion and memory in personality*. New York, NY: Free Press.

Spence, D. (1982). *Narrative truth and historical truth: Meaning and interpretation in psychoanalysis*. New York, NY: Norton.

Spitzer, R., Williams, J. M. G., Gibbons, M., & First, M. (1989). *Structured clinical interview for DSM III-R*. Washington, DC: American Psychiatric Publishing.

Sroufe, L. A. (1996). *Emotional development: The organization of emotional life in the early years*. New York, NY: Cambridge University Press. doi:10.1017/CBO9780511527661

Stern, D. (1985). *The interpersonal world of the infant*. New York, NY: Basic Books.

Teasdale, J. D. (1999). Emotional processing, three modes of mind, and the prevention of relapse in depression. *Behaviour Research and Therapy, 37*, S53–S77.

Toukmanian, S. G. (1992). Studying the client's perceptual processes and their outcomes in psychotherapy. In D. L. Rennie & S. G. Toukmanian (Eds.), *Psychotherapy process research: Paradigmatic and narrative approaches* (pp. 77–107). Thousand Oaks, CA: Sage.

Warwar, S. H. (2005). Relating emotional processing to outcome in experiential psychotherapy of depression. *Dissertation Abstracts International: Section B. Sciences and Engineering, 66*(1-B), 581.

Warwar, S., & Greenberg, L. S. (2000). Advances in theories of change and counseling. In S. D. Brown & R. W. Lent (Eds.), *Handbook of counseling psychology* (3rd ed., pp. 571–600). New York, NY: Wiley.

Watson, J. C., Gordon, L. B., Stermac, L., Kalogerakos, F., & Steckley, P. (2003). Comparing the effectiveness of process–experiential with cognitive–behavioral psychotherapy in the treatment of depression. *Journal of Consulting and Clinical Psychology, 71*, 773–781. doi:10.1037/0022-006X.71.4.773

Watson, J., & Greenberg, L. (1996). Emotion and cognition in experiential therapy: A dialectical–constructivist position. In H. Rosen & K. Kuelwein (Eds.), *Constructing realities: Meaning making perspectives for psychotherapists*. New York, NY: Jossey-Bass.

Watson, J. C., & Rennie, D. L. (1994). Qualitative analysis of clients' subjective experience of significant moments during the exploration of problematic reactions. *Journal of Counseling Psychology, 41*, 500–509. doi:10.1037/0022-0167.41.4.500

Westra, H. (2004). Managing resistance in cognitive behavioral therapy: The application of motivational interviewing in mixed anxiety and depression. *Cognitive Behaviour Therapy, 33*, 161–175. doi:10.1080/16506070410026426

White, M. (2004). Folk psychology and narrative practices. In L. Angus & J. McLeod (Eds.), *Handbook of narrative and psychotherapy: Practice, theory, and research* (pp. 15–52). Thousand Oaks, CA: Sage.

White, M. (2007). *Maps of narrative practice*. New York, NY: Norton.

Williams, J. M. G., Barnhofer, T., Crane, C., Hermans, D., Raes, F., Watkins, E., & Dalgeish, T. (2007). Autobiographical memory specificity and emotional disorder. *Psychological Bulletin, 133*, 122–148. doi:10.1037/0033-2909.133.1.122

INDEX

Abandonment, 31, 64, 74
ABM. *See* Autobiographical memory
Abuse, 35, 36, 74
Acceptance
 and emotional productivity, 19
 self-, 24
 symbolization for enhancing, 141
Actions, 46, 63
Action tendencies, 9, 24, 75
Actualizing, 6
Adams, K., 15
Adaptive emotional regulation, 6
Adaptive emotions
 activation of, 24, 105
 and actualizing tendency, 6
 defined, 5
 and empty stories, 67, 69
 meaning making from processing, 51
 primary. *See* Primary adaptive emotions
 and same old stories, 66
 symbolization of, 42
 transforming maladaptive emotion to, 7, 24, 30, 32, 52
 and unstoried emotions, 70, 71
Adolescence, 12
Affect. *See also* Emotions
 painful, 36
 synthesis of cognition and, 6, 141
 unstoried, 27
Affection, 91
Affective dysregulation, 35, 37
Affect labeling, 21
Affect regulation, 35. *See also* Regulation; Therapist empathic attunement
Agency. *See* Personal agency
Alliance ruptures, 42
American Psychological Association (APA), 53
Amygdala, 21
Anger, 30, 31
Angus, L., 14, 21, 22, 24, 27, 39, 42, 46, 50, 53, 54, 89, 99, 123
Anxiety, 45
Anxiety disorders, 31

APA (American Psychological Association), 53
Approach emotions, 7–8
Attachment. *See also* Therapist empathic attunement
 in healing stories, 93
 as impetus for storytelling, 38
 insecure, 36
 research on, 38
 sustaining sense of, 35
 and trauma, 120
Attending, 19
Author, client as, 89
Autobiographical memory (ABM)
 and depression, 97–98, 109, 113, 116
 embedding emotional states with, 70
 experiencing emotion shifts with, 52
 in healing stories, 91, 94
 and organization of memories, 140–141
 in same old stories, 63, 64
 in self-identity change stories, 89
 specificity of, 4
 and therapeutic bond, 26–27
 in trauma case analysis, 123
 of untold stories, 84, 85
Autobiographical memory narratives
 descriptions of, 8
 disclosure of, 45, 48, 49, 51, 64
 and emotional arousal, 15
 emotions in, 12
Autobiographical reasoning
 defined, 25
 as meaning-making activity, 45
Automated processing, 50
Autonomic nervous system, 23
Avoidance, of emotion
 and facilitating emotion themes, 28, 29
 overgeneral memory representation as, 98
 and unstoried emotions, 69
Awareness, 7, 9, 20, 26–28

157

Barrett-Lennard, G. T., 38, 39
Beliefs, 51
Betrayal, 31, 74
Blame, 102
Bodily felt sense
    awareness of emotions with, 20, 21
    and empty stories, 67
    focusing interventions for
        engaging, 105
    meanings based on, 33
    in retelling of stories, 64
    in unexpected outcome stories, 87
Bond, therapeutic. *See* Therapeutic bond
Boritz, T., 15, 98, 99
Bouffard, B., 21, 54
Bouffard-Bowes, B., 123
Bowlby, J., 38
Broken stories, 73–79
    defined, 59
    in depression case analysis, 109–112, 114, 115, 117
    emotional incoherence in, 61, 73–78, 109, 110
    narrative incoherence in, 78–79
    overview, 61
    and trauma, 73, 74, 120, 122–123, 128
    in treatment of depression, 105–106
Bruner, J. S., 3, 12, 140
Bryntwick, E., 75, 78, 99–105

Caregivers, 35, 36, 38
CBT (cognitive behavioral treatment), 13
CC (client-centered) treatment, 13–15
Change
    research on, 13
    in self-identity change stories, 89–91
    story, 23–24
    in unique outcome stories, 87, 88
Childhood experiences, 35, 74
Children, narration by, 36
Client-centered (CC) treatment, 13–15
Client engagement, 42, 54
Clients
    internal voice of, 6–7
    leading and following by, 6
Clinical depression, 106. *See also* Depression
Closure, 120
Coeditor, psychotherapist as, 26

Cognition
    synthesis of affect and, 6, 141
    in unexpected outcome stories, 87
Cognitive behavioral treatment (CBT), 13
Cognitive constructivist psychotherapy, 4
Cognitive-experimental research, 97
Cognitive markers, 97
Cognitive theory, 7
Coherence
    enhanced sense of, 7
    maintenance of, 142
    narrative, 109
    self-, 47, 75, 76, 98
    and trauma, 120
Combs, G., 33
Compassion, 30
Conceptual processing of emotions
    experiential processing vs., 21
    generation of self-reflections by, 23
Confidence, 47
Conflict splits, 10
Congruence, 19
Consolidation, of stories, 32–33
Constructionism, 33
Contentment, 88
Contrast, in storytelling, 27
Core beliefs, 42
Core emotion themes
    awareness of, 63
    evocation, exploration, and articulation of, 28–30
    in same old stories, 63, 64
Corrective relational experience, 42
Couples distress, 7. *See also* Significant others
Critic, experiencing self vs., 6–7
Cultural norms, 86, 90

Death, 74
Delight, 87
Depression, 97–118
    and autobiographical memory, 97–98
    clinical case analysis, 106–117
    effectiveness of EFT for treating, 7, 13–15
    EFT clients recovered from, 75

and innovative moments, 89–90
narrative-emotion perspective on, 97–98
and problem markers, 98–106
and same old stories, 63
shame and sadness in, 31
Dialectical–constructivist model, 19–34. *See also specific headings*
  awareness and contextualization of emotions in, 20
  bonding, narrative unfolding, and awareness phase in, 26–28
  consolidation and narrative reconstruction phase in, 32–33
  emotion and narrative processes in, 4
  evocation, exploration, and articulation of core emotion themes phase in, 28–30
  identity reconstruction in, 24–25, 32
  meaning and sense of self in, 13
  meaning making in, 19–25
  narrative construction in, 22–23
  story change in, 23–24
  symbolizing emotions in, 21–23
  transformation of emotion and development of new story outcomes phase in, 23–24, 30–32
Differentiation. *See also* Symbolization
  for activating primary adaptive emotions, 77
  defined, 5
  and embodied feeling states, 21
  and emotional productivity, 19
  as key strategy, 58
  for overcoming emotional incoherence, 75
  of positive and distinctive interpersonal experiences, 87
  transformation of emotion and story outcomes in, 23–24
  transition from storytelling to, 51
  in trauma case analysis, 122–123
Disclosures, client, 26–28. *See also specific types of disclosures, e.g.,* Untold stories
  creating safe space for, 143
  as fundamental to personal change, 58
  impediments to, 113

of memories and life events, 47–49
of narratives from autobiographical memory, 41, 45, 48, 49, 64
sensing inner experience of, 39
of significant relationship events, 52–53
and therapeutic bond, 42
of traumatic events, 49–50
Disconnected experiences, 3
Discrete events, 11–13. *See also* Micronarratives
Distress states, 23
Divorce, 74
Dominant internal voices, 67
Dominant narratives, 73
Dread, 45
Dysfunction, 6
Dysregulated emotional states, 69–70

EFT. *See* Emotion-focused therapy
Embodiment, human, 142. *See also* Bodily felt sense
Emotional arousal
  appropriateness of, 69
  deepened, 4
  in empty-chair task interventions, 54
  as goal of task interventions, 52
  heightening of, 32
  research on, 14–16
  and same old stories, 63
  in trauma case analysis, 122
  undifferentiated states of, 21
Emotional awareness, 7
Emotional change, 13, 24
Emotional differentiation. *See* Differentiation
Emotional expression, 69
Emotional health, 23
Emotional incoherence, 61, 73–78, 109, 110
Emotional processing, 23
Emotional productivity, 19
Emotional responding, 30
Emotional transformation, 112–115, 127–128
Emotion-focused therapy (EFT), 4–17. *See also specific headings*
  early development of, 4
  goals in, 7
  instrumental emotions in, 7, 8

Emotion-focused therapy, *continued*
  marked-guided interventions in, 6, 9–10
  meaning making in, 6, 10
  narrative perspective in, 11–13
  primary adaptive emotions in, 7–8
  primary maladaptive emotions in, 7–8
  purpose of, 9
  research on, 9, 13–16
  secondary emotions in, 7, 8
  treatment outcomes with, 13–16, 145
Emotion regulation. *See* Regulation
Emotions. *See also specific headings*
  in experience of self, 6
  in stories, 4
Emotion-schematic episodic memory structures, 31
Emotion schemes, 5, 141
Emotion shifts, 52
Emotion themes, 28–30
Empathic attunement, therapist. *See* Therapist empathic attunement
Empathic reflections, 64–65, 115
Empathic validation, 10
Empathy
  in empty-chair task intervention, 54
  self-, 45
  therapeutic, 38. *See also* Therapist empathic attunement
  in trauma case analysis, 123
  in treatment of depression, 102, 105
Emplotment, 140
Empty-chair interventions
  for activating primary adaptive emotions, 77
  for embedding emotional states in narratives, 72
  goals of, 52
  overview, 6, 7
  for repairing broken stories, 122
  sample dialogue, 93–94
  and self-identity, 53–56
  in trauma case analysis, 126–128
  and unfinished business, 10
Empty stories, 66–69
  defined, 59
  overview, 60
  and therapist empathic attunement, 37
  in treatment of depression, 104–105, 112
Engagement, client, 42, 54
Episodic memory, 31, 97, 98
Evolution, 142
Existential theory, 7
Experiencing, 15
Experiencing self, 6–7
Experiential beginning point, 71
Experiential engagement, 104
Experiential focus, 15
Experiential processing, of emotions, 21
External environments, 47
Externalizing, of events, 86
Externalizing interventions, 72
External narrative mode, 47–48, 51, 54
External narrative sequences, 14, 51

Family members, 63
Fear
  and memory, 31
  in same old stories, 64
Focusing, 10
Focusing interventions, 67, 105
Following, 6
Forgiveness, 123
Freedman, J., 33
Future events, 98

Gaps, in stories, 78, 79. *See also* Narrative incoherence
Gendlin, E. T., 20
Generalized patterns of actions, 63
Gestalt psychotherapy, 6, 7, 53
Goals, 51
Gonçalves, M., 89, 90
Goodman, P., 6
Greenberg, L. S., 16, 50, 89, 99, 137
Grieving, 30
Guiding, 6

Harber, K. D., 50
Harlow, H., 38
Healing stories, 91–94
  as opportunities for interventions, 144
  overview, 83
  in trauma case analysis, 134
Health, 23
Hefferline, R. F., 6
Here-and-now perception, 23

Human embodiment, 142
Humiliation, 105
Hurt, 31

Identity. *See also* Self-identity
  development of, 12
  formation of, 6
  sense of, 3
Identity reconstruction
  creating new perspectives on, 75
  in dialectical–constructivist model, 24–25, 32
  methods for, 136
  and same old stories, 66
Image maintenance, 23
Immune functioning, 23, 50
I-moments (innovative moments), 89–90
Implicit self-soothing, 29
Infants, 35
Injuries, interpersonal, 7
Inner peace, 88
Innovative moments (i-moments), 89–90
In-session change, 145
In-session problem states, 6
Insight, 42
Instrumental emotions
  assessment of, 7
  overview, 8
Intentions, 51
Internal environments, 47
Internal narrative mode, 49–51
Internal narrative sequences, 14, 51
Internal voices, 6–7
Interpersonal conflict
  EFT for treatment of, 13
  events associated with, 11
Interpersonal experiences, 87
Interpersonal injuries, 7
Interpersonal interactions, 73
Interpersonal maladaptive patterns, 99, 103, 108
Interpretations, 33
Interruption, of emotional experience, 29
Interventions
  empty-chair. *See* Empty-chair interventions
  externalizing, 72
  focusing, 67, 105
  marker-guided directive, 6, 9–10, 143. *See also* Narrative markers
  task, 52
  two-chair, 6, 7, 10, 52, 56–58, 77
Intrapersonal experiences, 87
Intrapersonal maladaptive patterns, 99, 103
Introjects, 6, 23
I positions, 7

Janis, L., 12

Kagan, F., 24, 42

Language
  creating personal experiences with, 3
  and empty stories, 68
  of same old stories, 62, 63
  symbolizing emotions with, 21–22, 141–142
  writing about emotional experience, 23
Lewin, J., 21, 51
Lieberman, M., 21
Life challenges, 140
Life events
  autobiographical memories of, 97
  broken stories of, 73
  children's narration of, 36
  disclosure of, 47, 49–50
  in empty stories, 68
  experiencing new responses to, 32
  facilitating reexperiencing of, 48
  memories of, 31
  reengagement with, 46
  relationship between interpretations and, 33
  and symbolizing emotions, 21, 23
  and therapist empathic attunement, 37
Life stories. *See also* Narratives
  development of, 12–13
  positive transformations in, 89
Limbic regions, 21
Lived experiences, 36
Lived story, 5
Long-term memory, 141
Loss, 74, 105, 120, 140
Love, 91

Macaulay, H., 39
Macronarratives
    beliefs about self contributing to, 51
    classification of narratives as, 47
    defined, 5, 13
    development of, 12
    as guiding standards, 32
    in narrative processes model, 47
    training for identifying, 145
Major depressive disorder, 106, 107. *See also* Depression
Maladaptive emotions. *See also* Unstoried emotions
    defined, 5
    in dysfunction, 6
    in empty-chair task interventions, 54
    experiencing of, 141
    meaning of, 24
    and memory, 31
    primary, 7–8, 70, 71, 113, 117
    in same old stories, 63–65
    shifting to adaptive emotions from, 7, 24, 30, 32, 52
    and treatment of depression, 104
    unstoried emotions as, 69–71
Maladaptive patterns, 99, 103, 108
Marker-guided directive interventions, 6, 9–10, 143. *See also* Narrative markers
McAdams, D., 12
McLeod, J., 27, 33
Meaning making
    and construction of self-identity, 45–46
    in dialectical–constructivist model, 19–25
    heightening of, 9
    options for, 47
    from processing adaptive emotions, 51
    as product of human activity and agency, 33
    in reflexive narrative mode, 50
    role of emotion in, 6
    and same old stories, 66
    for unstoried emotions, 70
Meaning-making markers, 81–95
    defined, 5
    in depression case analysis, 113
    healing stories, 83, 91–94, 134, 144

unique outcome stories, 82–83, 86–91, 111, 144
    untold stories. *See* Untold stories
Memory(-ies). *See also* Autobiographical memory narratives
    disclosure of, 47–49
    in empty-chair task intervention, 54
    episodic, 31, 97, 98
    gaps in, 78
    giving form to, 3
    long-term, 141
    restorying of, 54
Memory reconsolidation, 31
Memory reconstruction, 84
Mendes, I., 89, 90
Metaphor phrases, 53, 66
Micronarratives
    classification of narratives as, 47
    defined, 5, 13
    processing of, 32
    training for identifying, 145
Moment of a reconceptualization, 90

Naming, of emotions, 21–22
Narrative change, 13
Narrative coherence, 109
Narrative construction, 22–23
Narrative-emotion tasks, 145
Narrative-emotion training, 145
Narrative incoherence
    as block to narrative formulation, 29
    in broken stories, 78–79
Narrative-informed emotion-focused therapy, 11–13, 19. *See also specific headings*
Narrative markers. *See also* Meaning-making markers; Problem markers
    defined, 26
    in depression case analysis, 109
    and empty-chair task interventions, 54
    identification of, 104
    as indicators for type of intervention to use, 143–144
Narrative ordering, 140
Narrative Processes Coding System, 98
Narrative processes model, 46–52
    external narrative mode, 47–48, 51, 54

internal narrative mode, 49–51
reflexive narrative mode, 50–51, 54
shifting between modes, 51–52
Narrative reconstruction, 32–33
   in depression case analysis, 115–117
   with self-identity change stories, 89
   and therapist empathic reflections, 42
   in trauma case analysis, 134–136
Narratives. *See also specific headings*
   defined, 3
   emotional change with, 24
   as process diagnostic tool, 4
Narrative scaffolding, 5
Narrative schema, 25
Narrative sequences, 14, 51
Narrative Therapy (DVD), 53
Narrative unfolding, 10, 26–28
Negative emotional images, 21
New story outcomes. *See* Story outcomes, new
Nonverbal behavior, 88, 122

Open-ended questions, 53
Others, 51. *See also* Significant others
Overregulation, emotional, 69

Pace, of storytelling, 27
Painful emotions
   accessing and expressing, 54
   in broken stories, 73
   evocation of, 28–29
   organizing of client's, 36
   regulation of, 36
Paralinguistic cues, 88
Parents, 36. *See also* Caregivers
Past
   contrasts between present and, 90
   and self-understanding, 13
Past behavior, 87
Pellowski, Anne, 19
Pennebaker, J. W., 23, 50
Perceptual process, 14
Perls, F., 6
Personal agency
   and emotional productivity, 19
   enhancement of, 76
   with identifying your emotions, 9
   and meaning, 33
   meaning making as evidence of, 25

promotion of, 7
and same old stories, 62, 66, 104
symbolizing and reauthoring for creating, 139
therapeutic bond for enhancing, 39, 40
in unique outcome stories, 88
Personal narratives, 5. *See also* Narratives
Personal safety, 120
Person-centered theory, 7
Physical health, 23
Plotlines
   in broken stories, 59, 61, 73, 75, 76, 106
   changes in, 24, 32
   positive transformations in, 89
   in same old stories, 60, 63, 66
   tracking of, 38
   in unstoried emotions, 70
Positive change, 42
Positive emotions, 91
Posttraumatic stress disorder, 31
Primary adaptive approach emotions, 7–8
Primary adaptive emotions, 7–8
   activation of, 77
   for articulating coherent stories, 75
   shifting from maladaptive emotions to, 7–8, 30, 52
   shifting from secondary emotions to, 24
   and treatment of depression, 104
   and unstoried emotions, 70, 71
Primary maladaptive emotions, 7–8, 70, 71, 113, 117
Problematic reactions, 10
Problem markers
   defined, 5
   and depression, 98–106
   types of, 9–10, 59–62. *See also specific problem markers*
Process, methods of, 144
Process experiential therapy, 13
Process markers, 5
Process–outcome research, 14–15
Productive emotional arousal, 16
Prompting clients, 101
Psychodynamic therapy, 4, 7, 14
Psychotherapy
   cognitive constructivist, 4

Psychotherapy, *continued*
   as discursive activity, 3–4
   gestalt, 6, 7, 53
Psychotherapy research, 97

Qualitative methods/measures, 144

Reason, 46
Reauthoring, 89, 105, 139
Recollective experience, 31
Reconceptualization moments, 89–90
Reconsolidation period (memory), 31
Reexperiencing, 63
Reflection, on emotion, 6, 23, 64–65.
   See also Self-reflection
Reflexive narrative mode, 50–51, 54
Reflexive narrative sequences, 14
Reflexive processing
   activation of, 22
   productive, 21
   and understanding of experience, 47
Regulation
   client capacity for, 36, 42
   and emotional productivity, 19
   enhancement of, 27
   integrating emotional and narrative processes as, 28
   of painful affect, 36
   and reflection on emotion, 23
   skills for, 7
   symbolization for enhancing, 141
   of underregulated emotion, 21
   and unstoried emotions, 69, 70, 72
Relapse prevention, 13
Relationship events, 52–53
Relationships, therapist–client, 6
Repetition, in storytelling, 27
Reported speech dialogue, in storytelling, 27
Responding, emotional, 30
Restorying, 11, 33, 54, 75. *See also* Narrative reconstruction
Retelling
   bodily felt sense from, 64
   reexperiencing vs., 63
Ribeiro, A., 89, 90
Rogers, C. R., 6, 38
Role-play interactions, 25, 53, 70, 72, 122. *See also* Empty-chair interventions; Two-chair interventions

Rotondi-Trevisan, D., 21
Rumination, 98

Sadness
   with depression, 31
   emotional shifts from, 30
   and memory, 31
   in same old stories, 64
Safety, 120
Saint-Exupéry, Antoine de, 5
Same old stories, 62–66
   challenging assumptions of, 87
   defined, 59
   and healing stories, 93
   overview, 60
   and storytelling rhythm, 27
   transformation of, 141
   in treatment of depression, 98–105, 107–110
Sarbin, T., 4
Scaffolding questions, 36–37, 53
Scripts
   emotion, 5
   in same old stories, 60, 63
Secondary emotions
   defined, 8
   in depression case analysis, 117
   shifting to primary emotions from, 24
   underregulated emotions as, 69
Secondary reactive emotions, 7
Security, 3, 91
Self
   compassion for, 30
   continual construction of, 25
   creating new perspectives on, 75
   emotionally differentiated account of, 12
   experiencing, 6–7
   in reflexive narrative mode, 51
   sense of, 3, 11–13
   views of, 42, 51, 54, 89, 91, 122. *See also* Introjects
Self-acceptance, 24
Self-coherence, 47, 75, 76, 98
Self-construction, 140
Self-critical processes
   challenging of, 25
   two-chair interventions for addressing, 56

Self-empathy, 45
Self-esteem, 30
Self-identity, 45–58
    construction of, 46–51, 140
    continual construction of, 46
    damage to, 142
    and empty-chair interventions, 53–56
    external narrative mode for constructing, 47–48
    internal narrative mode for constructing, 49–50
    long-term memory as basis for, 141
    narrative processes model for change in, 46–52
    positive views of, 42
    reflexive narrative mode for constructing, 50–51
    and retelling significant relationship events, 52–53
    and two-chair interventions, 56–58
Self-identity change stories, 83, 89–91
Self-identity narratives, 86–87
Self-interruptive splits, 10
Self-mastery, 42
Self-narrative, 12, 47. *See also* Narratives
Self-narrative reconstruction, 4. *See also* Narrative reconstruction
Self–other schematic structure, 54
Self-reflection
    in depression case analysis, 115–117
    generation of, 23
    heightening of, 9
    narrative as space for, 140, 141
    as outcome of therapist empathic attunement, 42
    therapeutic bond for enhancing of, 39
    in trauma case analysis, 134–136
Self-soothing, 29, 45
Sense making, 27
Sense of self. *See also* Self-identity
    construction of, 46
    empty, 36
    origins of, 140
    in unexpected outcome stories, 87
Sensorimotor processing, 23
Separation, 74
Shame, 8, 31, 64, 105
Significant others
    in healing stories, 91–94
    placing blame on, 102
    role-play interventions for confronting, 53–54
    unfinished business toward, 10
    views of, 54, 122
"Sneaky poo" treatment, 72
Social constructionism, 33
Social problem solving, 98
Somaticizing, of problem, 104
Soothing
    empathic, 45
    by parents, 36
    self-, 29, 45
Sousa, I., 89
Specific autobiographical memory, 5
Stories, 3, 4. *See also* Narratives
Story change, 23–24
Story integration, 75
Story outcomes, new
    in depression case analysis, 112–115
    facilitating development of, 30–32
    and transformation of emotion, 23–24
    in trauma case analysis, 127–134
Storytelling
    rhythm of, 27
    transition to emotional differentiation from, 51
Students, narrative-emotion training for, 145
Suicide, 121, 124
Surprising events, stories about. *See* Unexpected outcome stories
Symbolization
    of adaptive emotions, 42
    for creating agency, 139
    defined, 5, 9
    in dialectical–constructivist model, 21–23
    and emotional productivity, 19
    in empty stories, 67
    for enhancing emotion regulation, 141
    of primary emotions, 70
    in same old stories, 66
    techniques for, 52
    by therapist, 72
    verbal, 141–142
Systematic evocative unfolding, 10

Task analysis, 144
Task interventions, 52
Teasdale, J. D., 98
Therapeutic alliance
   and client disclosures, 26–27
   development of, 39, 45
   and empty-chair task interventions, 54
   quality and strength of, 37
Therapeutic bond, 26–28, 38, 39, 42, 113
Therapeutic empathy, 38. *See also* Therapist empathic attunement
Therapist(s)
   guiding to internal narrative mode by, 21
   as important contributor, 19
   leading and following by, 6
   roles of, 15, 26, 143
Therapist-client relationships, 6
Therapist empathic attunement, 36–45
   clinical outcomes of, 42
   and emotional disclosures, 52–53
   and empty stories, 66
   experience and expression of, 37–39
   importance of, 36–37
   to previously avoided emotions, 71
   sample dialogues, 39–44
   soothing with, 29
   stages of, 38–39
   in trauma case analysis, 124
   in two-chair task interventions, 56
   to untold stories, 84
Told stories, 5
Training, narrative-emotion, 145
Trauma, 119–137
   and broken stories, 73, 74, 120, 122–123, 128
   clinical case analysis, 123–136
   in depression case analysis, 113
   effectiveness of EFT for treating, 7
   emotional disclosure of, 49–50
   events associated with, 11
   narrative-emotion perspective on, 120–121
   as source of affective dysregulation, 35–36
   and unstoried emotions, 72
Treatment outcomes
   with EFT, 14–16
   narrative and emotion processes for effective, 11
   and narrative processes model, 52
Trust
   and client disclosures, 26
   in healing stories, 91
   and painful personal memories, 36
Truth, 33
Two-chair interventions
   for activating primary adaptive emotions, 77
   goals of, 52
   overview, 6, 7, 10
   and self-identity, 56–58

Unclear felt sense, 10
Underregulation, emotional, 21, 69
Unexpected outcome stories, 82–83, 87–89, 111
Unfinished business markers, 10
Unfolding, narrative, 10, 26–28
Unique outcome stories, 86–91
   as opportunities for interventions, 144
   overview, 82–83
   self-identity change stories, 83, 89–91
   unexpected, 82–83, 87–89, 111
Unproductive emotional arousal, 16
Unstoried affect, 27
Unstoried emotions, 21, 59, 61, 69–72
Untold stories, 81, 84–86
   as block to narrative formulation, 29
   in depression case analysis, 108–113
   as opportunities for interventions, 144
   overview, 82
   in trauma case analysis, 123–124

Verbal symbolization, 141–142
Voice quality, in storytelling, 27
Vulnerability, 10

Warmth, 91
Well-being, 7
White, Michael, 4, 72
Withdrawal emotions, 7
Witness, psychotherapist as, 26
Words, symbolization with, 21–22, 141–142

Working alliance, 38
Worry, 98
Worth, conditions of, 6
Writing, 23

York I Depression Study
    and autobiographical memory, 15
    case analysis of dyads from, 63
    poor outcome therapy dyad from, 78
    recovered client case example from, 97, 106
    same old story narratives in, 99
    successful vs. unsuccessful EFT treatments in, 21
    unique outcome stories in, 87, 88
York Unfinished Business Study, 121

ABOUT THE AUTHORS

Lynne E. Angus, PhD, CPsych, is a professor of psychology at York University in Toronto, Canada, and is currently president of the Society for Psychotherapy Research. She is the senior editor of *The Handbook of Narrative and Psychotherapy: Practice, Theory, and Research* (2003) and coeditor of *Bringing Psychotherapy Research to Life: Understanding Change Through the Work of Leading Clinical Researchers* (2010). Dr. Angus's psychotherapy research program focuses on the contribution of narrative and emotion processes for productive treatment outcomes in emotion-focused therapy. Dr. Angus codeveloped the narrative processes model and coding system with Heidi Levitt and Karen Hardtke. Finally, Dr. Angus is an active clinical practitioner and psychotherapy supervisor who is committed to furthering the integration of psychotherapy research and practice in community-based settings.

Leslie S. Greenberg, PhD, is distinguished research professor of psychology at York University in Toronto, Canada. He is a leading authority on working with emotion in psychotherapy and the developer of emotion-focused therapy, an evidence-based approach. He has authored and coauthored the major texts on emotion-focused approaches to treatment of individuals and couples, including *Emotion-Focused Therapy for Depression* (2005); *Emotion-Focused Therapy: Coaching Clients to Work Through Their Feelings* (2002); *Facilitating Emotional Change: The Moment-by-Moment Process* (1996); and *Emotion-Focused Couples Therapy: The Dynamics of Emotion, Love, and Power* (2008). Dr. Greenberg has received the Distinguished Research Career Award of the Society for Psychotherapy Research, an international interdisciplinary society, as well as the Carl Rogers Award of the American Psychological Association's Society for Humanistic Psychology. He also has received the Canadian Council of Professional Psychology Programs' Award for Excellence in Professional Training and the Canadian Psychological Association's Professional Award for Distinguished Contributions to Psychology as a Profession. He is a founding member of the Society of the Exploration of Psychotherapy Integration and a past president of the Society for Psychotherapy Research. He conducts a private practice for individuals and couples and trains people in emotion-focused approaches.